Rock & Roll SAXOPHONE

By JOHN LAUGHTER

Foreword by SCOTT PAGE

Basic techniques include; The Growl, Flutter Tone, Altissimo Register, Reed Squeal, Double Tone, Slap Tongue, Note Bending and Sliding, Trill, Vibrato, Subtone, Staccato and Special Effects. Over 25 Photos and Biographies from 1955 through the 1990's. Special Guest performances on tape by Myanna, Jenny Hill and The Burning Brass.

2nd Edition

Recorded at Kudzu Recording Studio, Macon, Ga.
John Laughter - Saxophones, Narration
Dwayne Boswell - Keyboard, Percussion, Bass, Guitar
Tim Griggs - Producer

Cover Photo of Scott Page
Courtesy of Scott Page
Photographer Armando Gallo

Walt Tucker Group
5225 San Fernando Road West
Los Angeles, CA 90039

ISBN 0-931759-36-6
SAN 683-8022

Faces

Contents

About the Author 3

Foreword by Scott Page 4

CD Track List 5

Introduction 6

LESSON ONE – **The Growl** 7

    Great Horns of America by Bob Ackerman 10

    Lee Allen 13

LESSON TWO – **Flutter Tone** 14

    Sil Austin 15

LESSON THREE – **Altissimo Register** 16

Altissimo Fingering Chart 19

    The Burning Brass 20

    Jenny Hill 21

    Sam Butera 22

LESSON FOUR – **Reed Squeal** 24

Making Reeds Last Longer 24

    Dave Camp 25

    The Champs 26

LESSON FIVE – **Double Tone or "Doo Wop"** 27

    Angella Christie 33

    Clarence Clemons 34

LESSON SIX – **Slap Tongue** 35

    Johnny Colla 36

    King Curtis 37

LESSON SEVEN – **Note Bending and Sliding** 38

    Steve Douglas 40

    The First Saxman 42

    Richard Elliot 43

LESSON EIGHT – **Trill** 45

    Kenny G 46

    Little Richard and Grady Gaines 47

LESSON NINE – **Vibrato** 48

    Herbert Hardesty 49

    Johnny & The Hurricanes 50

LESSON TEN – **Subtone** 51

    Dave Koz 53

    Amy Lee 55

LESSON ELEVEN – **Staccato** 57

    Joe McGlohon 58

    Myanna 59

    Boots Randolph 60

    Billy Vaughn 61

LESSON TWELVE – **Special Effects** 62

    Jr. Walker 63

Special thanks to:

MIX Bookshelf - MIX Magazine (Blair Jackson, Mr. Bonzai), Bibb Music Center (Art and Paula Motes, Billy, Boudleaux, Jimmy, Jolene, Larry, Ralph), Evans Music Company (Marilyn Gay), Larry Fennelly - Macon College, The Grapevine (Donnie Brooks, Derek Darity, Jerry Dowd, Jim McLendon, Larry McLendon, Tommy West, Dave Rickard, Sharon Wilhelm, Mark King, Robin Hughes, Tom Wilson), Dieter Hennies (Germany), Mike Hammett - Tracks/Record Bar - Macon, GA, Saxophone Journal (Ken Dorn, David J. Gibson, Nina Santoro), David Kellogg, Jim Macklin, Fletcher Barnes, Dr. Glenda Earwood-Smith - Macon College Saxophone Quartet, Art McClure (Sun City, AZ), Dora McCrary - Typeset, Cliff Meyers, Ron Middlebrook - Centerstream Publications, Arthur Moore - Studio 26, Julius Nieder, Lenn Palmer (Galesburg, IL), Rico Products, Philip Rovner - Rovner Products, L. A. Sax (Pete LaPlaca, H. Allan), Play It Again Sam's - Macon, GA, (Jimmy and Clifton McDonald), David Schurer (Atlanta), Ray Stevens - Clyde Records, Norman "Rocky" Short - Middle Georgia Wind Ensemble, A. Hammond Scott - Black Top Records, Tommy West - Photographer, The Atlanta Saxophone Shop - Keith Epperson, Jr., Windplayer Magazine - Michelle Margetts, Paige Henson - Macon Magazine (Lynn Stovall Cass and Joni Williams Woolf) and my friends at GEICO who were so helpful in locating CD liner notes - Daniel Miller - Windplayer - Michael and Martha Fennell Violins - Macon.

Very special thanks to:

Scott Page, Bob Ackerman, The Burning Brass, Jenny Hill of The Burning Brass, Sam Butera, Dave Camp, Angella Christie, Johnny Colla, Steve Douglas, Herbert Hardesty, Dave Koz, Amy Lee, Joe McGlohon, and Myanna.

For Lee, Amy and Julie, with love and appreciation.

John began playing saxophone in 1956 after hearing Clifford Scott's solo on the hit record, *Honky Tonk* by the Bill Doggett Combo. Other inspirations followed; Lee Allen and Grady Gaines (Little Richard), Herb Hardesty (Fats Domino), Sam Butera (Louis Prima), Sil Austin, Johnny and the Hurricanes, Billy Vaughn and The Champs. Rock 'n Roll and Rhythm and Blues was sweeping the nation. John began playing nightclubs in 1959 and continued to perform while in the United States Air Force (1963-1967). In 1973 he graduated from the University of South Florida, Tampa, Florida with a degree in instrumental music education and taught public school band for ten years. While in college, John performed in classical, pop and jazz ensembles including jazz concerts with Don Ellis, Maynard Ferguson and Dizzy Gillespie. In addition to symphonic and marching band, he built public school stage band programs in Pinellas County, Florida and Atlanta, Georgia. John continues to perform in a variety of musical groups including a nine piece show band playing music of the 50's, 60's and 70's, a variety combo, The Middle Georgia Wind Ensemble (community band), and for the classical touch, the Macon College Saxophone Quartet.

Author's Equipment

Model	Mouthpiece	Ligature	Reed
Tenor-Selmer MK Seven	Rovner "Deep V"#10-RAM40	Rovner	Rico Plasticover
Alto-Selmer-Pro USA	Rovner "Deep V"#7-RAM40	Rovner	Rico Plasticover
Soprano-Power Beat	Rovner "Deep V" #7-RSM30D	Rovner	Rico Plasticover
Baritone-Conn	Berg Larsen 100/2, Hard Rubber	Rovner	Rico Plasticover

Rovner Products, P. O. Box 4116, Timonium, MD 21093

Sennheiser 421 and Shure Wireless 98 Microphones, Peavey Ultraverb Digital Effects Processor, Peavey EQ 31 - 1/3 Octave Graphic Equalizer.

-Foreword -

Creating your own sound is, in my opinion, the number one aspect of your playing career. It is also the hardest to achieve. Having your own unique style is as important if not more important than your technique.

This book and the accompanying tape gives the player the beginning basics for experimenting with his or her sound. It will start you thinking about the possible effects that can be created with your instrument. When you practice try playing each exercise with different dynamics and attitudes. First play as loud as you can and then as soft as you can. Combine and experiment with these effects in all keys to help you develop your own playing personality. One note played with the right attitude can be more powerful than a dazzling display of notes. Remember, it ain't what you play it's what you say. So good luck and keep it simple.

Scott Page

SCOTT PAGE

A twenty year veteran of the music and entertainment industries, his music career includes music preparation, composing, arranging and conducting for various musical productions. He co-wrote the country hit "Too Many Times", recorded by Anita Pointer (Sisters) and Earl Thomas Conley. The tune went to #2 on Billboard's Hot Country Singles Chart and was the title cut of an Earl Thomas Conley album.

Scott performed on the 1989 Pink Floyd European/Soviet Union Tour. Additional tours have included: Pink Floyd 1987-1988 world tour, Toto, Supertramp, Duran Duran, Diana Ross and others. He has also played in numerous music videos, studio sessions and live performances.

In 1989 Page founded The Walt Tucker Group, a full service production facility encompassing all aspects of an artist's image and concept development including record and video/film production, promotion and merchandising.

CD Track List

(Studio music by Boswell and Laughter)

1. Introduction
2. <u>Lesson One</u> – **The Growl**
3. <u>Lesson Two</u> – **Flutter Tone**
4. *Big Dogs* (P. Calo – Tater Music, BMI) Performed by Myanna. Produced by Peter Calo and Myanna. Engineered by Bob Patton. Recorded at Thin Ice Productions Studio. 1992, all rights reserved. Bridge City Music, P.O. Box 25 Boston, MA 02130.
5. <u>Lesson Three</u> – **Altissimo Register**
6. <u>Lesson Four</u> – **Reed Squeal**
7. <u>Lesson Five</u> – **Double Tone or "Doo Wop"**
8. <u>Lesson Six</u> – **Slap Tongue**
9. *Come Falling Down* – Performed by The Burning Brass of Brooklyn, New York featuring Lillian Jackson – lead vocal, Pam Fleming – trumpet, Jenny Hill – sax and Nilda Richards – trombone. Recorded in New York, all rights reserved.
10. <u>Lesson Seven</u> – **Note Bending and Sliding**
11. <u>Lesson Eight</u> – **Trill**
12. *Sarah's Dance* – Performed by Myanna from her CD *Myanna* on Bridge City Music Records.
13. <u>Lesson Nine</u> – **Vibrato**
14. <u>Lesson Ten</u> – **Subtone**
15. *Passion* – Written and performed by Jenny Hill
16. <u>Lesson Eleven</u> – **Staccato**
17. <u>Lesson Twelve</u> – **Special Effects**
18. Conclusion

Photo's –Biographies Alphabetical Order

Scott Page – foreword 4
Bob Ackerman 10
Lee Allen 13
Sil Austin 15
The Burning Brass 20
Jenny Hill of The Burning Brass 21
Sam Butera 22
Dave Camp 25
The Champs 26
Angella Christie 33
Clarence Clemons 34
Johnny Colla 36
King Curtis 37
Steve Douglas 40
The First Saxman 42
Richard Elliot 43
Kenny G 46
Grady Gaines 47
Herbert Hardesty 49
Johnny & The Hurricanes 50
Dave Koz 53
Amy Lee... 55
Joe McGlohon 58
Myanna 59
Boots Randolph 60
Billy Vaughn 61
Jr. Walker & The All Stars 63

INTRODUCTION

This study is intended for the student who wants to learn the basic introductory techniques of obtaining the various sounds and effects used by many performing saxophonists in the field of Rock and Roll, Jazz, Blues, Fusion and Country. These techniques can be used individually or in combinations which produce certain effects to enhance your solo performance.

It takes years of experience to "pick up" these techniques, however this study guide and cassette tape will enable a student to understand these effects within a short period of time.

In addition to the practice time involved in this study guide, the student must realize that he or she still needs the basic understanding of the principals of tone, technique and music theory. Behind every outstanding saxophone soloist in the field of Pop music one will always find a solid understanding of music theory.

Although it is not the intention of this study to endorse any particular brand name of instrument, mouthpiece or reed, it must be understood that in the area of special effects a performer must have an instrument, mouthpiece and reed combination which will enable one to produce these effects. One of the best sources of obtaining information regarding equipment is to read various music publications such as *Downbeat, Saxophone Journal* and *Windplayer* which include interviews with professional artists. *Contemporary Saxophone* by John Laughter (published by Centerstream), also contains a detailed list of equipment used by many of today's finest saxophonists. Another avenue of education is to discuss equipment with local experienced saxophonists who play regularly and perform Top-40, Blues, Jazz, Fusion or Country styles.

Some of the best sax players perform at a L.A. SAX show

GROWL

Our lessons of special effects for a saxophonist begin with the most common of all effects, the growl.

Very early recordings of blues bands and big bands show that saxophonists were using this particular effect in the early days of popular music. The growl is commonly referred to as the "strained" or "scratchy" sound used by many blues musicians.

In 1955 (the official birth year of Rock and Roll), 1956 and 1957, there were many Top 40 hits which featured a saxophone solo;

1955

Tweedle Dee - LaVerne Baker	2/55
Mambo Rock - Bill Haley & the Comets	3/55
Birth Of The Boogie - Bill Haley/Comets	3/55
Rock Around The Clock - Bill Haley/Comets	7/55
Razzle-Dazzle - Bill Haley/Comets	7/55
Ain't That A Shame - Pat Boone	8/55
Ain't That A Shame - Fats Domino	8/55
At My Front Door - El Dorados	10/55
Burn That Candle - Bill Haley & the Comets	11/55
Rock-A-Beatin' Boogie - Bill Haley/Comets	11/55
When You Dance - Turbans	12/55

1956

See You Later Alligator - Bill Haley & the Comets	2/56
Tutti Frutti - Little Richard	2/56
Why Do Fools Fall In Love - Frankie Lyman & The Teenagers	3/56
R-O-C-K - Bill Haley & The Comets	4/56
The Saints Rock 'n Roll - Bill Haley & The Comets	4/56
Long Tall Sally - Little Richard	5/56
My Blue Heaven - Fats Domino	5/56
Long Tall Sally - Pat Boone	5/56
Slippin' And Slidin' - Little Richard	6/56
I'm In Love Again - Fats Domino	6/56
When My Dreamboat Comes Home - Fats Domino	7/56
Ready Teddy - Little Richard	7/56
So Long - Fats Domino	8/56
Rip It Up - Bill Haley & The Comets	9/56
Honky Tonk - Bill Doggett Combo	10/56
In The Still Of The Night - Five Satins	10/56
Rudy's Rock - Bill Haley & The Comets	11/56
Blueberry Hill - Fats Domino	12/56
Slow Walk - Sil Austin	11/56
Slow Walk - Bill Doggett Combo	12/56

1957

Jim Dandy - LaVerne Baker	2/57
Blue Monday - Fats Domino	2/57
Come Go With Me - Dell-Vikings	4/57
I'm Walkin' - Fats Domino	4/57
It's You I Love - Fats Domino	6/57
So Rare - Jimmy Dorsey	6/57
Young Blood - Coasters	7/57
Jenny Jenny - Little Richard	7/57
C. C. Rider - Chuck Willis	7/57
Whispering Bells - Dell-Vikings	8/57
Short Fat Fannie - Larry Williams	8/57
Diana - Paul Anka	8/57
Mr. Lee - Bobbettes	9/57
Keep A Knockin' - Little Richard	10/57

Many of these solos used various amounts of the growl. However, on October 7, 1957, in #8 position on *Billboard* was **Little Richard's** *Keep A Knockin'* which was featured in the movie *Mr. Rock 'n Roll*. The saxophone section consisted of Clifford Burks (tenor), Wilbert Smith (tenor), Grady Gaines (tenor), and Samuel Parker, Jr. (bari.). The tenor solo on this hit record was, by far, the most forceful growl used to date. And, the growl in this solo was exceptionally effective because it was used in the upper register. It represented power, energy and excitement which was heard on jukeboxes, airways and sock hops across the nation.

The effect of the growl is best utilized in the upper range of the instrument, generally from G above the staff and higher. The effect is easier to handle in the higher range. Although you can produce a growl in the middle range around third space C and lower, the effect becomes somewhat garbled.

Good _____ Better _____ Best

A growl is produced by humming while playing a note. Although that may sound easy enough it's a little more complicated because of the coordination involved. The best way to learn the approach to the growl is to have the reed and mouthpiece attached to the neck pipe but have the neck pipe removed from the body of the saxophone.

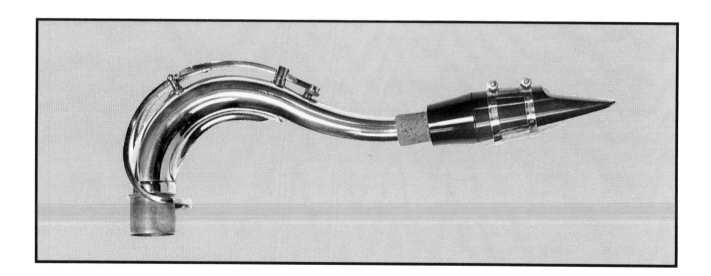

Begin blowing through the neck pipe and periodically hum. You will be able to hear yourself hum and you will also hear the effect this is having on the sound that you are producing through the neck of the saxophone. After you have practiced this for a period of time, attach the neck piece to the saxophone and play the following notes; A, C, B, and D and hum periodically in order to achieve the sound.

EXAMPLE 1

EXAMPLE 2   EFFECTIVE RANGE

BEST ....

EXAMPLE 3   PLAY WITH CLEAR TONE THEN REPEAT WITH GROWL

You need to be aware that your embrochure might be altered while using this technique. There may be a tendency for your lower lip to sag slightly which will make the intonation go flat. Always listen to make sure that the pitch stays in tune.

The popularity of the growl has continued throughout the years. The following recent hits feature sax solos which use various amounts of the growl;

Rockin' At Midnight - Honeydrippers
Livin' Right - Glenn Frey
Seasons Change - Expose
Waiting For A Star To Fall - Boy Meets Girl
Living In America - James Brown
You Got It All - Jets
Diggin' Your Scene - Blow Monkeys
Hungry Eyes - Eric Carman
Foolish Beat - Debbie Gibson
Love On A Rooftop - Desmond Child
How Will I Know - Whitney Houston
I'll Always Love You - Whitney Houston
What Becomes Of The Broken Hearted - Paul Young
Take It Back - Reba McEntire

Bob Ackerman

The
GREAT HORNS OF AMERICA

A BUSINESS DEVOTED TO THE RECYCLING & REGENERATION OF THE SAXOPHONES OF THE EARLY 20TH-CENTURY CRAFTSMEN

BY BOB ACKERMAN

In the 42 years I have devoted to the study of music, I have played thousands of instruments. Having been educated in the 50's, I naturally was introduced to the instruments of that period first. They were the models being sold in the stores and were touted as the best ever. If you went to your local music store today and looked at the new models, you would probably hear a similar story.

My first good horns were a 1956 Conn 6M alto and a 1953 Martin Committee tenor, and they played great. But Mark VI Selmers were the rage and by 1957 I needed them to fit into the sax sections I was working in professionally.

On two separate occasions I did the switch with my teachers - alto, Joe Soldo, then two years later tenor, Joe Allard. I missed the Conn and Martin, but I hung in there and went with the trend, even when my friends complained that something had happened to my sound. For 25 or 30 years I played this pair of VI's.

In the early 80's, as my mouthpiece business (begun in the 70's) developed and expanded, I began to deal in horns. Today I am not under the peer pressure of those sax sections whose sound was controlled down to the reed as well as the mouthpiece. I am also no longer a commercial musician trying to fit into someone else's mold. Thus I am free to play whatever and however I wish. This opportunity, coupled with a worldwide interest in vintage equipment, has now placed me back in time to the 20's and 30's for most of the instruments I use.

This is an experience that is still constantly evolving but seems well rooted in concept. It is opening many new doors for me both in business and music. The process of instrument making has changed from the craftsman and his hand tools, to the craftsman and his machines, to the machines and their operators, to the machines and their computers. This transformation has taken more than a century and represents the dehumanization of musical instruments. Older instruments seem more resonant, more flexible in pitch and sound, and more individualistic in general. No two are alike! Doesn't this sound like jazz?

The instruments of today sound oppressively identical. Their pitch is fixed on a center that cannot move easily. This becomes painfully obvious in performances, whether in the N.Y. Philharmonic or the Basie Band, when these fixed-pitch models fail to keep up with the shadings and nuances of the older movable-pitch instruments. The result: collision.

How did we get to this point? Here's a quick historical overview:

1920's

CONN: A medium-weight body. The King of Jazz- all brass and reeds in the Jimmie Lunceford orchestra played Conns. (Lunceford was Count Basie's original model.) Conn made gold-plated custom models as did most of the companies.

BUESCHER: A lighter-weight body. Mr. Buescher was a foreman with the Conn company. Both instruments influenced and mixed with one another. Buescher had a sweeter sound than Conn. Today there is a cult of Americans following Siguard Rauscher who use these instruments (primarily 1925-1940 models).

MARTIN: A heavy-wall sax with soldered tone holes and some heavy wailing sounds. Mr. Martin was also at one time an employee of Conn.

KING: Not yet big in saxes in the 20's.

HOLTON: Made a Rudy Weidoff model with very detailed mechanism.

SELMER: Was only starting to appear.

1930's

CONN: The absolute Jazz King, played by Pres and Bird. Conn changed models: 6M Alto, 26M Conquerer Alto (custom made), 10M Tenor, 30M Tenor (custom made), 12M Bari.

BUESCHER: Developed the Aristocrate, which had a still sweeter sound.

KING: Developed the Zephyr, a very modern design, light in body weight. This horn became very popular.

MARTIN: Made the Handcraft model, which represented the dark sound.

SELMER: Started with the Cigar Cutter model, which was used by the more commercial bands (Glenn Miller, etc.) and just before the war came out with a fancier model called the Balanced Action.

1940's - 1950's

The war stopped almost all production for many years. By 1947 things began to happen again, but American companies faced heavy competition from cheap European labor. The Americans still tried, then sputtered, gasped, and gave way to Selmer. Student instruments were now their thing as school bands rose in popularity.

KING & MARTIN: King developed the Super 20, Martin developed the Committee Models. The more individualistic jazzers, such as Cannonball Adderly, Bird, Johnny Griffin, Jackie McClean, all played Kings. Budy Tate played the Martin.

SELMER: Marketed a much fancier looking horn with a slick, fast mechanism to boot. Selmer brought out first the Super Balanced Actions Nos. 47000-54000, then the Mark VI. They clearly gained control of a monopoly on the pro sax market. From here on we all know the story pretty much.

1960's - 1970's

SELMER: The Mark VI was made from 1956-1975, when worn tooling and the changing of the guard in the Selmer family brought on a new model--the Mark VII, a more wide-open, stronger-blowing horn with a change in key design and a larger bore. By 1980 the bright VII was again changed to the dark Super Action 80.

1980's

YAMAHA: Appeared with model 61's, then 62's, and now the 825's, etc.
YANAGASAWA: Produced finely-made instruments with silver body and bell.
KEILWORTH (COUF): Made heavy-walled, drawn tone hole saxes with the same chimney on the tone hole as 30's Conns with a lip on the top.
BUESCHER & KING: Resembled Selmers with no lip on top of the chimney.

AS YOU EXPERIMENT with these older great horns of America you must bear in mind a few things. Their mechanisms are simple and must be set in the original fashion to work at their best. Appropriate pads and mouthpieces must also be used. Players who cross idioms to make a living - playing jazz, legit, and/or commercial - will need not only a selection of mouthpieces but also a few different axes.

I personally have my VI's for commercial section work and a set of Conns (20's-30's) for creative playing. There is nothing like these great horns of America to give you the raw, individual character a jazz player should have.

Remember that key height and correct size pads are critical. The exact height of the keys should always be set by your repairman with you personally playing the horn with the mouthpiece you have selected for it. There can be a variation of 1-3 mm in heights depending on you. If anything is off, pitch and response will suffer.

Incidentally, flutists face the same question: whether to play a modern fixed-pitch axe or go with the older, more flexible models. They like Louie Lot (1880's-1920's), Haynes (20's-60's), and Powells (30's-60's). Clarinetists have fewer options, as wood is not long lasting. Many players still prefer Selmer Balanced Tone and Centered Tone models. Buffett players often look for 70,000-100,000.

If you wish to explore these instruments, please contact me, as they are a big part of my work. Also, please note that I am not saying there is no place for modern instruments. They do commercial music the best. In business I handle everything and feel we must be flexible to survive.

Bob Ackerman
15 McGotty Place
Irvington, NJ 07111

LEE ALLEN

In the 1950's, **J and M Studio** in New Orleans put together one of the finest session bands in the history of Rock and Roll, and Rhythm and Blues. This band consisted of;

Lee Allen - tenor sax
Alvin "Red" Tyler - baritone sax
Earl Palmer - drums
Edgar Blanchard - guitar
Justin Adams - guitar
Huey "Piano" Smith - piano
James Booker - piano
Frank Fields - bass

Specialty Record files indicate that Lee Allen and Alvin "Red" Tyler played on the following hits by **Little Richard** which had a major influence on young saxophonists everywhere: *Tutti Frutti, Slippin' and Slidin', Miss Ann, I Got It, Hey-Hey-Hey-Hey, Rip It Up, Ready Teddy, Heeby-Jeebies, All Around the World, Can't Believe You Wanna Leave, Shake A Hand, Jenny Jenny, Good Golly Miss Molly, Baby Face, By the Light of the Silvery Moon, The Girl Can't Help It* and *Send Me Some Lovin'*.

Lee Allen also joined forces with the legendary Herb Hardesty on the following hits by **Fats Domino**; *Ain't That A Shame, When My Dreamboat Comes Home, Blueberry Hill, My Blue heaven, I'm Walking* and *Valley of Tears*. Lee Allen also recorded a successful album in 1958. His hit single *Walking With Mr. Lee* reached #54 on national charts. Lee Allen continues to perform with **The Blasters** in Los Angeles, California. His solo style will be a major influence for generations to come.

Photo courtesy Warner Brothers Records - "The Blasters"

FLUTTER TONE

By now you have begun the first study of special effects for the saxophonist with the use of the growl. Our next lesson will deal with the "flutter tone". In the process of learning this particular effect you should be prepared to ruin several reeds. Because of the rapid movement used by the tip of the tongue, you will normally damage the tip of the reed until experience takes it course.

Only the tip of your tongue is used. Before practicing with the mouthpiece, hold a mirror in front of your face and observe the following; the tip of the tongue is placed against the roof of your mouth, just behind your top front teeth. Exhale quickly and forcefully to activate the rapid "up and down" movement of the tip of your tongue. As your tongue moves it makes short dents in the air flow which produces the same effect on the tone of your saxophone.

An excellent example of this technique was performed on a 1958 recording titled *Tequila* by the Champs on Challenge Label #1016. A 1988 recording by George Harrison, *Got My Mind Set On You* on Dark Horse Record #2817807 also features a tenor using this effect. **At this time please refer to lesson two on the cassette tape.**

EXAMPLE 4

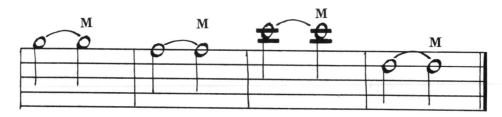

EXAMPLE 5

One of the first Top 40 hits to feature this technique was *Honky Tonk Part 2* by the **Bill Doggett Combo** on King label #4950 in 1956. Saxophonist Clifford Scott altered his fourth solo with "flutter tongue" which was very effective for this blues style instrumental hit. Others followed;

1958	*Rebel Rouser*	Duane Eddy
1958	*Cannonball*	Duane Eddy
1959	*Forty Miles of Bad Road*	Duane Eddy
1962	*Twistin' the Night Away*	Sam Cooke
1965	*Shotgun*	Jr. Walker & The All Stars

And, more recently,

1989	*Every Beat of My Heart*	Taylor Dayne

SIL AUSTIN

Sil Austin was born in 1929 in Donellon, Florida and is a very well known R&B tenor saxophonist. He played with the **Tiny Bradshaw Orchestra** before forming his own band. While under contract with Mercury Records, he recorded thirty-two albums. His first Top 40 hit was *Slow Walk* in 1956 which reached #17 for seven weeks. *Danny Boy* was his second hit which reached #59 in 1959 for twelve weeks and the recording *Plays Pretty for the People* is now considered a classic. For those who really enjoy ballads and the beauty of the "subtone", you will appreciate the artistry of Sil Austin.

Photo courtesy Mercury-Polygram Records #832351-4 Q-1.

ALTISSIMO REGISTER

Altissimo playing will be a more difficult technique to master.

Altissimo notes are very popular in today's pop music. It is seldom that you hear a solo on an alto or tenor saxophone in the Top-20 that does not use at least one altissimo note. A 1988 recording entitled *Waiting For A Star To Fall* by Boy Meets Girl on RCA 8691.7 features an alto saxophone solo in which the artist uses several altissimo notes. More outstanding examples can be heard on solos by David Sanborn, Marc Russo and Dave Koz. This technique will be impossible to obtain unless you have the correct mouthpiece and reed combination which enables you to produce the effect. Generally speaking, if you have a small opening between the tip of the mouthpiece and tip of the reed then you will need a strong reed to produce this effect. On the other hand, if you have a large tip opening then you can use a softer reed in comparison. A weak reed used with a small tip

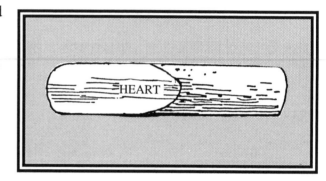

opening will not produce an altissimo note. The reed will simply close under pressure and the air flow will stop. Gradually increase the strength of your reed and use a medium open mouthpiece. The combination of the right reed and mouthpiece and the force of the lower jaw pushing upward toward the heart of the reed will be the key to success.

You can find many fingering charts which are available for this register. Some of the fingering will work well on the alto, some on the tenor. You will also find that different brands of saxophones produce different degrees of volume and intonation problems in the altissimo range. Your success in this area will depend upon the combination of your reed, mouthpiece, brand of instrument and amount of daily practice. Please refer to **Contemporary Saxophone** by John Laughter which is published by Centerstream Publications for additional information on equipment.

The following recent hits feature one or more altissimo notes used by the soloist;

> *I'm Not In Love* - Will To Power
> *Endless Summer Nights* - Richard Marx
> *Seasons Change* - Expose
> *Living In America* - James Brown
> *Digging Your Scene* - Blow Monkeys
> *Hip To Be Square* - Huey Lewis & The News
> *Hit Me Like A Hammer* - Huey Lewis & The News
> *Love Is A Wonderful Thing* - Michael Bolton
> *Heart On The Line* - Richard Marx
> *How Will I Know* - Whitney Houston
> *Shelter Me* - Cinderella
> *Tell Me What You Dream* - Restless Heart

You can obtain more information from the following books: *Beginning Studies in the Altissimo Register* - R. Lang, *Studies in the High Harmonies* - T. Nash and *Saxophone High Tones* - E. Rousseau.

In order to introduce you to these notes we will begin with high A. It is recommended that you approach the first altissimo note much like a trumpet player produces octave intervals during warm-up. We will use the same approach by starting with low A (second space) followed by high A (first line above staff) followed by the high A altissimo note.

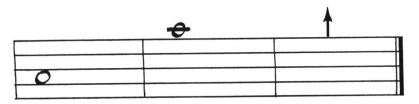

EXAMPLE 7

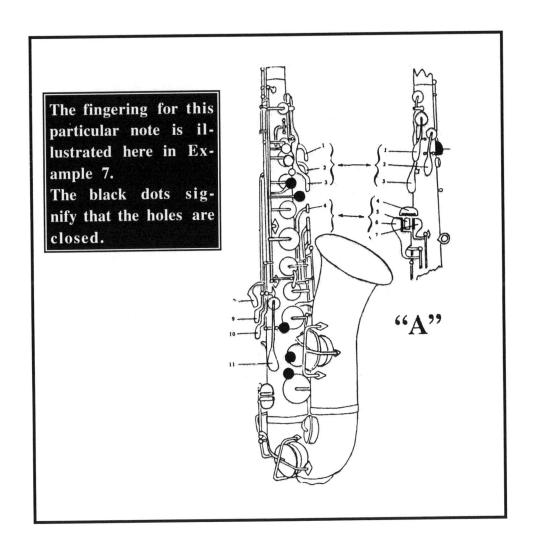

The fingering for this particular note is illustrated here in Example 7.
The black dots signify that the holes are closed.

"A"

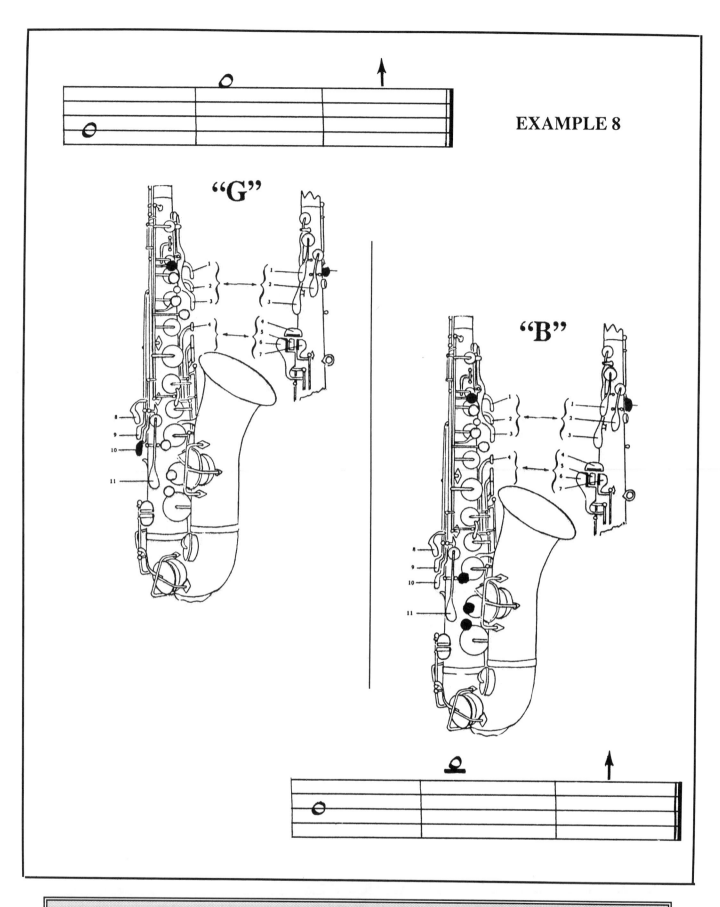

EXAMPLE 8

"G"

"B"

At this time please refer to lesson three of your study guide cassette tape.

Altissimo Fingering Chart

THE BURNING BRASS

THREE-PIECE FEMALE HORN SECTION

Pam Fleming - Trumpet, Jenny Hill - Sax, Nilda Richards - Trombone

ALSO AVAILABLE WITH BAND
AS AN EIGHT-PIECE
'REGGAE NOUVEAU' ENSEMBLE

PERFORMANCE CREDITS

Maxi Priest World Tour, 1992-93
        (Far East, South America, Caribbean)
Reggae Sunsplash 1991 World Peach Tour (U.S.)
        backing Maxi Priest, Shinehead, Dennis Brown,
        Andrew Tosh, Carlene Davis, Little Lenny
Burning Spear (1986-88), including World Tour
        (Africa, South America, Europe, Canada and U.S.)
Steppin' Razor (1985-87)
The Majestics (1987 JVC Jazz Festival)
Diahnne Abbott
Leroy Sibbles, Alton Ellis, John Holt

Featured artists,
Burlington (VT) Fifth Annual Reggae Festival (1990)

Winner,
Brooklyn Lager World Beat Competition 1990 (New York, NY)

RECORDING CREDITS

1990	-	"Reggae USA Compilation" (ROIR)
1989	-	"To Be Immortal," Oran "Juice" Jones (CBS)
1989	-	"Burning Spear Live in Paris" (Blue Moon Records) *
1988	-	"Mistress Music," Burning Spear (Warner Bros./Slash)
1987	-	"People of the World," Burning Spear (Warner Bros./Slash) *
1986	-	"Rebel Soul" (Studio One)
1986	-	"First Cut," Steppin' Razor (Breakthrough Prod.)

* Grammy-nominated

Jenny Hill
Saxophones, flute, piccolo

Performance Credits:
Active NYC free lancer in jazz, reggae, and latin music

Co-leader of Burning Brass
- Three-piece all-female horn section
- Eight-piece funky reggae band

1992 -93 Maxi Priest World Tour

Reggae Sunsplash 1991 Tour backing:
- Maxi Priest
- Shinehead
- Carlene Davis
- Dennis Brown
- Andrew Tosh

Burning Spear World Tours (1986-88):
- Africa
- Europe
- Canada
- South America
- Jamaica
- USA

Performances with:
- Daniel Ponce
- Bob Hope
- Robert Palmer
- Cab Calloway

Recording Credits:
1990 - *Reggae USA*, ROIR
1989 - *To Be Immortal*, Oran "Juice" Jones, CBS Records
1989 - *Living in Paris*, Burning Spear, Warner Brothers/Slash
1988 - *Mistress Music*, Burning Spear, Warner Brothers/Slash
1987 - *People of the World*, Burning Spear, Warner Brothers/Slash
1986 - *We Got the Feeling*, Wanda and the Way It Is, Island Records

Honors:
1990 - Brooklyn Lager World Beat Competition winner
1990 - Burlington VT Reggae Festival, featured artist
1986 - National Endowment for the Arts Jazz Studies Grant
1983 - Lennie Johnson Outstanding Musician Award and Scholarship (Berklee College)

Education:
1983 - Diploma in Music Performance, Berklee College of Music, Boston, MA
1978 - Classical flute major, Indiana University, Bloomington, IN

Equipment:
Tenor-Pro Model L.A. Sax and Selmer Mark VI with custom M/P by Francois Louis of Belgium and Rico Royal 3 1/2 reed Soprano - Yanagisawa and Muramatsu flute

Sam Butera

RECORDING - T.V. - MOTION PICTURE CREDITS
ALBUMS - WITH THE WILDEST
Cassette available:
Poor Boy Records - P. O. Box 42395 - Las Vegas, NV 89104

"The Big Horn"	"Thinking Mans Sax"
"Big Sax and Big Voice"	"The Rat Race"
"Wildest Clan"	"He's Number 1"
"Atlantic City Special"	"Play It Again Sam"
"Love Is In The Air"	"By Request"
"Body and Sax With A Little Soul"	"Live! Sheer Energy"
"A Tribute To Louis Prima" Part 1	

ALBUMS -
WITH LOUIS PRIMA AND KEELY SMITH

"The Wildest"	"Blast Off"
"Return of the Wildest"	"King of Clubs"
"Wildest at Tahoe"	"Jungle Book"
"Prima Show in the Casbar"	"Prima '75"
"Angelina"	"Prima Generation"

Recorded and did all the arrangements for an album with Sammy Davis Jr. called "SAM MEETS SAM. WHEN THE FEELING HITS YOU".

Also "STARGAZER" with Frank Sinatra, as well as all of the arrangements for Louis Prima and Keely Smith from 1954 on.

TELEVISION CREDITS

Johnny Carson Show	Dean Martin Show
Merv Griffin Show	Steve Allen Show
Jackie Gleason Show	Mike Douglas Show
Jerry Lewis Telethon	A Current Affair
David Letterman Show	Joe Piscopo Special
Paul Shaffer T.V. Movie "Viva Shaf Vegas" Plus many others..	

MOTION PICTURE CREDITS
"Hey Boy, Hey Girl" with Louis Prima
"The Rat Race" with Tony Curtis and Debbie Reynolds
"Twist All Night" with Louis Prima and June Wilkinson

SAM has been on the Playboy Magazine Jazz Poll as one of the top ten jazz musicians in the world.

by Bill Mears

The name SAM BUTERA is renowned as one of the most powerful instrumental vocalists of this or any other musical era. SAM, with his distinctively rocking voice and impeccable playing of the tenor sax has astounded millions of people via performances from Las Vegas' major showrooms to Julie Podell's famed Copacabana in New York City. He has reached and thrilled millions more with his recordings, T.V. and motion picture appearances.

SAM was born in New Orleans. At the age of eighteen, he was voted the Outstanding Teenage Musician in America by Look Magazine. Shortly after this award Sam worked with many of the big bands including Tommy Dorsey, Ray McKinley, Joe Richman, and in New Orleans, with Al Hirt.

Eventually, he formed his own group and recorded for RCA Victor, producing such hits as "Easy Rockin" and "Chicken Scratch".

In the early fifties, Sam joined Louis Prima and Keely Smith in Las Vegas, and the rest is musical history. Together they did recordings, T.V.shows, movies and broke attendance records in every showroom or lounge in the country.

Sam has appeared with Frank Sinatra all over America from Caesars Palace in Las Vegas to the Latin Casino in Philadelphia.

He recorded "Stargazer" with Mr. Sinatra which was written by Neil Diamond and released through Reprise records.

Sam has also appeared with Danny Thomas, Jerry Vale, Sergio Freanchi, Jimmy Roselli and Sammy Davis, Jr. with whom he recorded an album "When Sam Meets Sam, When The Feeling Hits You".

His latest appearances have been on the nationally acclaimed "A Current Affair" T.V. show and the "David Letterman Show". He appeared on Joe Piscapo's "Halloween Special", and a T.V. movie with Paul Shaffer called "Viva Shaf Vegas".

Sam has also been seen numerous times through the years with the "Jerry Lewis MDA Telethon".

SPOTLITE MAGAZINE

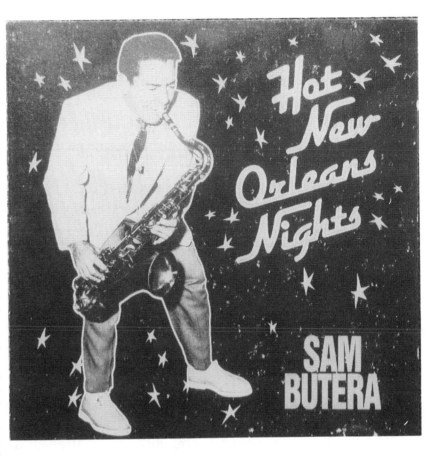

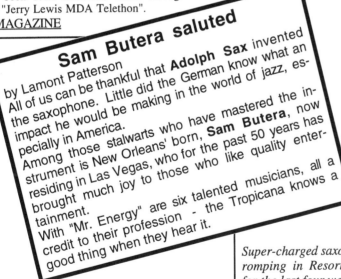

Sam Butera saluted

by Lamont Patterson

All of us can be thankful that **Adolph Sax** invented the saxophone. Little did the German know what an impact he would be making in the world of jazz, especially in America.

Among those stalwarts who have mastered the instrument is New Orleans' born, **Sam Butera**, now residing in Las Vegas, who for the past 50 years has brought much joy to those who like quality entertainment.

With "Mr. Energy" are six talented musicians, all a credit to their profession - the Tropicana knows a good thing when they hear it.

Sonny Schwartz

Super-charged saxophonist-vocalist Sam Butera has been stomping and romping in Resorts International Hotel-Casino's Rendezvous Lounge for the last four weeks, but he still can't believe his eyes. Or, his ears either, for that matter.

The Butera group has been attracting enthusiastic reviews and appreciative audiences since it opened here four weeks ago. But the reviews were extra-enthusiastic and the audience more wildly appreciative when a recent headliner at Resorts' Superstar Theater "sat in" with Butera after concluding his performance.

"It was really a kick when Frank (Sinatra) got up on stage with us the first time," Sam says of "Ol' Blue Eyes," who had recorded Neil Diamond's "Stargazer" with Butera. "Frank was in the Rendezvous enjoying himself and the next thing I know, he's up there kidding around and introducing us. "Then the next night, Frank came up and sang. It was a thrill, believe me. And the people in the lounge just went wild."

Butera says he's been "absolutely awed" by the enormous crowds that have been patronizing the casino and lounge at Resorts.

REED SQUEAL

The "reed squeal", as it is sometimes referred to, is perhaps the easiest effect to play on the saxophone and also the most unpredictable.

The reed squeal is generally used when the performer wants to play beyond the altissimo range. This technique will produce the highest sounds on the saxophone. The performer simply puts the bottom teeth next to the reed and continues to exhale producing the effect. The main difference between the reed squeal and the altissimo effect is that the player does not apply hard pressure to the reed with the teeth. One must be very careful since this can easily ruin a reed. This effect should probably be used sparingly because of the potential hazard done to the fiber of the cane by applying direct teeth pressure.

Of all the effects discussed in this study guide, the reed squeal is probably the most effective from the standpoint of audience appeal. Imagine, if you will, that the band is really kicking a rock tune and the crowd is dancing and having a great time . . . you begin your solo and end up holding a reed squeal at the end of your solo for fifteen seconds or longer! Rest assured . . . the crowd will respond!

Since this effect is somewhat unpredictable you must use extreme care in not moving your head, lower jaw or shoulders while using this technique. You will notice after limited practice that the frequency of the pitch will change with the slightest movement of pressure.

An early recording which features this effect is *Memphis Soul Stew* by King Curtis on Atco Record #33-231 (1967). Another recent hit which features this technique on alto is *Bad to the Bone* by George Thorogood.

Please refer to Chapter four of the study tape at this time.

HOW I MAKE REEDS LAST LONGER By Eric Kloss

Reprinted by permission from RICO Products

I have been using Rico reeds for twenty-seven years and have been seasoning them in the following way for twenty-five years. Without seasoning, the average life expectancy of a reed is from two to four weeks. This is because of saliva which breaks down the pores of a reed, destroying vibrancy and responsiveness. Reeds can last from two to three months if this play for curing your Rico reeds is used.

1. Moisten a reed taken from a box and play test it for over-all responsiveness. The reed should be slightly stiff without being too hard to play. When finished, place this reed in a LaVoz Reedgard to dry for at least a day.

2. The next day remove the reed from the Reedgard and place it in a full glass of water for twenty-five minutes. Play the reed for ten minutes. The reed should be a bit softer and more responsive, especially in the low register. Then, dry the reed again in the Reedgard for another day.

3. Repeat the seasoning process, step 2, by moistening the reed in water for twenty-five minutes, playing it for ten minutes and then drying it again in the reedgard for a day.

4. Play the reed again, this time for fifteen minutes. If it performs to your satisfaction, place it in a Reedgard for future use. Have several seasoned reeds in their Reedgards for ready playing. If the reed is still unresponsive, season it again, step 2.

5. When the seasoning is completed and the reed is responsive, keep it moist and flat between performances in a plastic Reedgard kept in a small zip-locked plastic bag for moisture retention. Be sure to wipe the reed thoroughly after each use with a soft cloth before returning it to the Reedgard.

Happy seasoning to you all.

DAVE CAMP

Dave Camp is a dynamic, versatile, saxophonist extraordinaire. Whether it is writing music for television (Bay Watch, Fashion Videos), doing sessions (Basia, Al Stewart, Peter White), composing music for music production libraries (Killer Tracks) or just jamming with Tower of Power, Dave Delivers! His latest CD is titled *From The Asylum* by the Windows (Blue Orchid - DA Music, #2014-2), P. O. Box 3, Little Silver, NJ 07739.

"Windows is a unique opportunity to play with great musicians who are also great friends... It shows in the music." Dave hails from Monterey, California and is currently residing in Venice with his wife of five years, Holly, and his 3 year old daughter, Olive.

B. M. BERKLEE COLLEGE OF MUSIC

PLAYED WITH:	SHARED STAGE WITH:		MISC. SESSIONS:	TOURS:
Al Stewart	Grover Washington	Walter Beasley	"Strawberry Road" - Japan	Al Stewart -
Peter White	Tom Scott	Ronnie Laws	"Ramona" - movie	U.S., Canada, England,
Jeffrey Osborne	Fourplay	Phillip Bailey	"Slaughter's Big Rip-Off" - movie	Japan, and Puerto Rico
Burt Bacharach	Ottmar Liebert		Seagrams, Labatts "Blue Light"	
Chuck Mangione	Rippingtons		Killer Track Production Music Library	
Doc Severinson	The Band		"Bay Watch" - TV	
Buddy Rich	Maria Muldaur		"Fashion Videos" - TV	
Grant Grisson	Dave Mason		Peter White - albums - "Excuse Moi" and "Reveillez-Vouz"	
			Al Stewart - album	
FESTIVALS:	ACTING:		Windows - album - "From the Asylum"	
Catalina Jazz Festival	Old Milwaukee Beer - "Beach Treasure"		Skipper Wise - album - "The Clock and the Moon"	
Monterey Jazz Festival	Mini-Series "Sinatra, The Early Years"			
Aspen Jazz Festival	Taco Bell			
Cambridge Folk Festival				

EQUIPMENT:

Tenor: Selmer Balanced Action (May 1940) with Brillhardt Level Air M/P. Tip of M/P has been opened and the chamber enlarged. 2 1/2 Rico Royal reeds and Winslow ligature for improved harmonics.

Alto: Selmer Mark VI (1964) with Meyer hard rubber M/P. Sax neck acoustically altered by "Oleg" in Los Angeles. Mouthpiece throat has been enlarged and a wedge has been built in for better high notes. 2 - 2 1/2 reeds.

Soprano: Selmer Mark VI with Selmer hard rubber M/P and #3 reeds.

RAMSA WMS2 clip-on microphone into a Yamaha Diversity Wireless Receiver.

THE CHAMPS

Lead guitarist Dave Burgess was head of A&R and the first artist signed to Gene Autry's Challenge label. He released three singles as "Dave Dupre" and a fourth under his own name, but all failed to chart. Then he recorded an instrumental, *Train to Nowhere*, with session musician Danny Flores on saxophone and piano. While recording instrumental tracks for a Jerry Wallace album, Burgess had some studio time left and decided to record a "B" side for *Train to Nowhere*. The musicians present included Flores, drummer Gene Alden, guitarist Buddy Bruce and bass guitarist Cliff Hils. Flores came up with a song he had written while visiting Tijuana. Burgess liked it, and suggested Danny shout "Tequila" in his low voice at the appropriate breaks. The track was considered a throwaway, and none of the musicians hung around the studio long enough to hear a playback. The group decided to use the name of Gene Autry's horse, Champion. **The Champs** were born. At the same time Danny Flores also changed his name using his middle name, Carlos, and his father's middle name, Del Rio. He came up with Chuck Rio. *Train to Nowhere* was released on 12/26/57 and went nowhere. DJ's started to play the "B" side, *Tequila*, which went #1 on the R&B charts for four weeks.

1958	#1	*Tequila*
1958	#30	*El Rancho Rock*
1958	#59	*Chariot Rock*
1960	#30	*Too Much Tequila*
1962	---	*Tequila Twist*
1962	#40	*Limbo Rock*
1962	---	*Limbo Dance*

Members:
Dave Burgess - lead guitar - Lancaster, California
Dale Norris - guitar - Springfield, Mississippi
Chuck Rio - sax - replaced by Jimmy Seals - Rankin, Texas
Ben Norman - bass guitar - replaced by Bobby Morris - Tulsa, Oklahoma
Gene Alden - drums - replaced by Dash Crofts - Cisco, Texas

Dave, Dale, Chuck, Ben and Gene originally formed the group and played around the West Coast area in the late fifties. After *El Rancho Rock*, Chuck Rio left the group to go on his own. Members Jimmy Seals and Dash Crofts became superstars.

DOUBLE TONE OR "DOO WOP"

This particular effect has been used in all forms of popular music for many years. The sound is most commonly associated with the use of a plunger on a trumpet or trombone bell as seen in the early big bands whereby the tone was altered by putting the plunger up to the bell, then moving it which produces an open and closed effect, hence "double tone". The term "Doo Wop" also comes from the same effect by closing and opening the bell. No doubt there are other terms for this technique.

In 1957, R&B singer/songwriter **Chuck Willis** released *C. C. Rider* (Atlantic 45-1130) which climbed the **Billboard** charts to #12. This hit record featured an excellent tenor solo which included the double tone technique. The saxophonist alternated between two third space C's on the "pick up" notes going into the solo and again on the fourth measure of the solo. As a result of this hit, many young performers became aware of this new technique. This was just another example of the early influence that Rock and Roll and Rhythm and Blues had on a new generation of saxophonists throughout the nation and around the world. Other early hits which featured this technique include;

1961   *I Like It Like That* - Chris Kenner
1961   *You Can't Sit Down* - Philip Upchurch Combo

EXAMPLE 9

Reg	Alt	Reg	Alt

On the saxophone this technique is done by alternating between two identical notes using different fingerings. One can refer to this as "alternate fingering". For example, the first and most obvious of the double tones is produced by playing the third space C then playing the same third space C by using the alternate fingering of low C and the octave key. Alternating between the two combinations of fingering will produce the double tone.

The pitch of the notes also determines how obvious the effect will be. Since the "alternate" note may be somewhat flat or sharp, this slight difference in tuning will help the overall effect. **Please refer to the study tape at this time.**

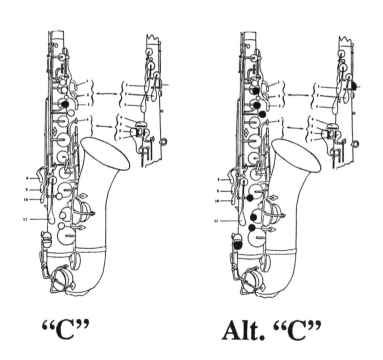

"C"   Alt. "C"

Please refer to the study tape at this time.

A second fingering which produces an obvious double tone will be the A above the staff. Play high A then continue to play it while you close right hand F, E and D fingers at the same time.

EXAMPLE 10

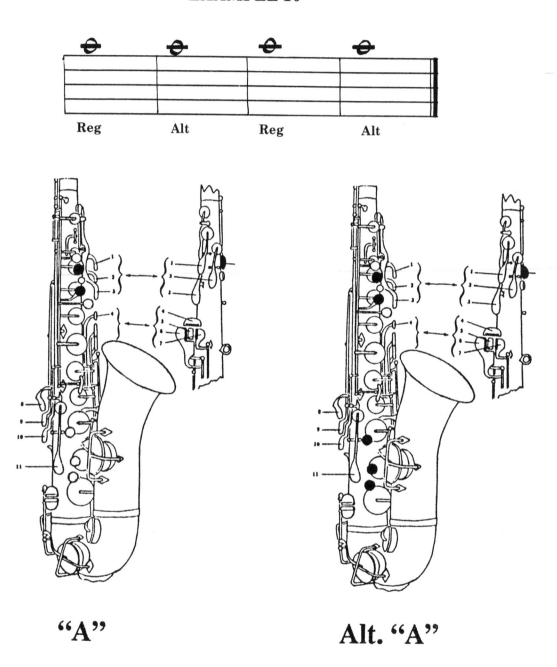

Reg   Alt   Reg   Alt

"A"   **Alt. "A"**

You will hear the effect of the change between the two A's. Practice opening and closing the right hand for this particular note and you will soon realize the value of producing these tones in solo work.

Two more notes which are commonly used with alternate fingering is fourth line D and fourth space E. The D is produced by alternating between the regular fingering of D and the side D key that would ordinarily be used with the octave key in order to produce high D.   Simply alternate between that D and the side D key under the left hand.

EXAMPLE 11

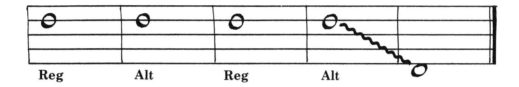

Reg   Alt   Reg   Alt

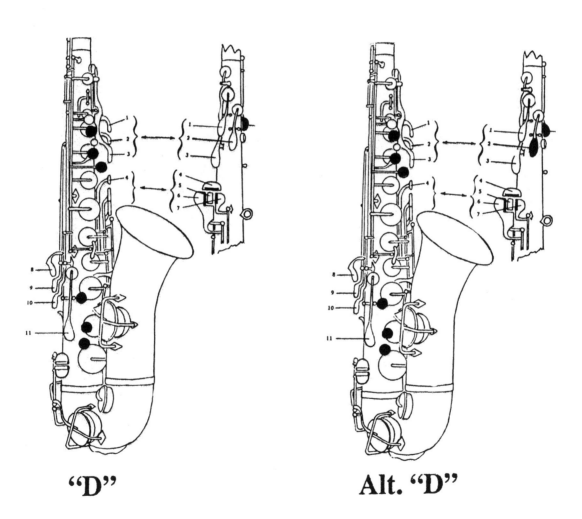

"D"   Alt. "D"

29

You can leave the right hand D, E and F fingers down if you desire. The advantage to this particular fingering will be discussed more in chapter seven since it lends itself well to sliding down to the low register from a D. Another option is to play only the side D key as illustrated.

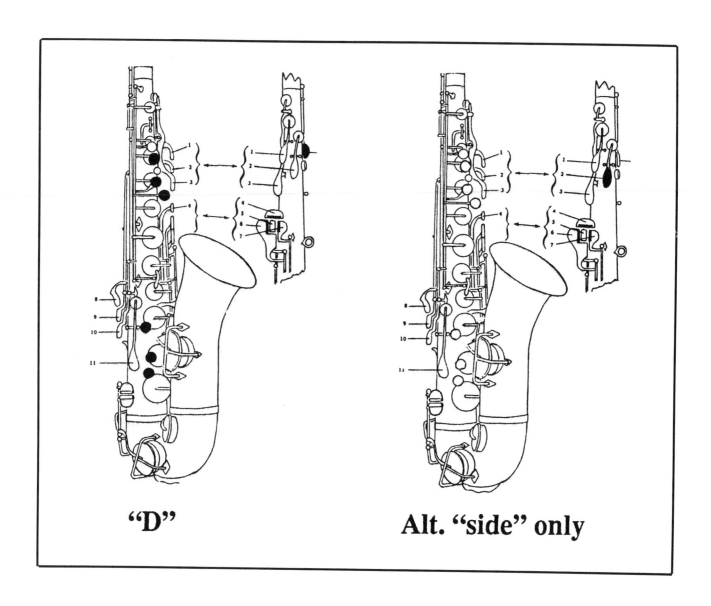

"D"   Alt. "side" only

Another note is fourth space E. Again use the regular E fingering then alternate over to the left hand E fingering that you would normally use in the high register. Don't forget the right side key for the correct high octave E fingering.

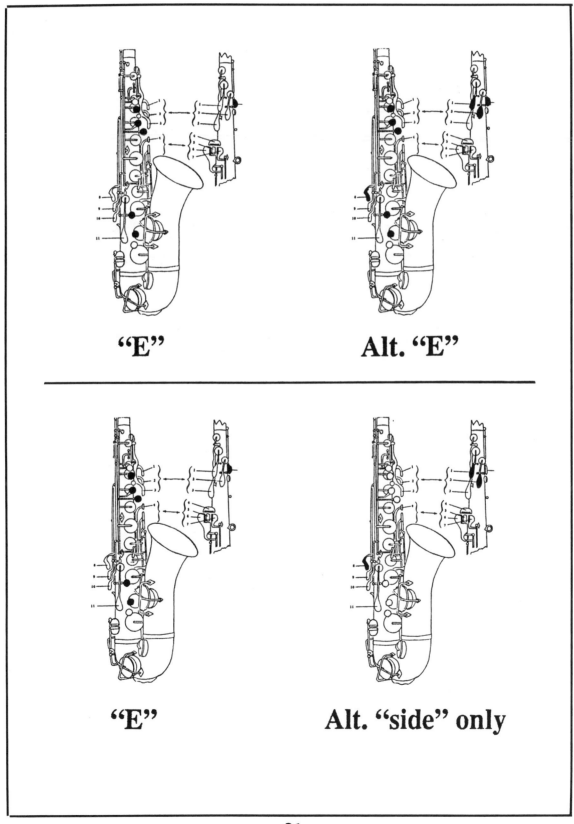

Alt. "E"

"E"

Alt. "side" only

With the use of the double tone there are many possibilities of altering tones. You should also take advantage of combining the double tone with lip bending and note sliding which will be covered in chapter seven. In many cases the effect will be enhanced greatly by the combination of several different techniques in one solo.

EXAMPLE 12

Please refer to chapter five of the cassette tape.

Another technique which produces a similar effect as the double tone is "dampening" the tone with your tongue, rather than using alternate fingering. This effect is produced by laying your tongue against a portion of the reed while holding the note and then releasing your tongue. Other names for this effect include "muffle tongue" and "ghosting". By "lightly" laying your tongue against the reed you will cut the volume in half and alter, or "dampen" the tone. For example, play a high A and alternate between blowing freely, and gently laying your tongue against the reed while you continue to blow. You can produce various degrees by dampening the first 1/3 of the reed, or all of the shaved portion.

Please refer to the cassette tape at this time.

Angella Christie

Angella Christie, a young gifted and phenomenal musician of the 90's, is a saxophonist extraordinaire. She has been an instrumentalist for more than eight years and has recorded professionally since 1985.

Angella graduated from the High School for Performing and Visual Arts in Houston, Texas and she holds a BA and BSW degree from Houston Baptist University. Ms. Christie is founder and principal of Angella Christie Sound Ministries, Inc. (ACSM), an organization she began after completing college. Angella's vision for ACSM is to give listeners the highest quality of Christian music in its purest form.

While pursuing her educational and professional goals she has always had energy to donate her time and talent to activities such as" Run-Away Hot Line, Family Connection (a youth shelter), Detroit Hunger Telethon, and Muscular Dystrophy Fundraiser.

As a saxophonist Angella has received numerous honors and awards. Some of these awards are: J. O. Patterson Fine Arts Scholarship, The Sealy Jazz All Star Band Certificate of Merit, Sealy Jazz Festival II at Sam Houston State University, 22nd Annual Jazz Festival, Special Award for Outstanding Musicianship, the Gospel Music Academy Awards of Texas Saxophonist of the Year - 1980 and 1981.

In the midst of her volunteer activities and receiving of awards, Angella has appeared professionally at notable events such as:

Tour of West Africa (1990) in Lagos, Nigeria, Kensington Temple in London, England, FORUM...Port of Spain, Trinidad, 700 Club Bread Basket, Brooklyn Academy of Music...New York, Atlanta Arts Festival, 1988 Tribute to Presidential Candidate Rev. Jesse Jackson, 1989 MLK Birthday Parace, Atlanta, GA., opening act in concert for: Bebe & Cece Winans, John P. Kee, Richard Smallwood Singers, Vanessa Bell Armstrong , and Al Greene. Additionally, Angella has been a featured artist at the National Baptist, Apostolic Church of God, Church of God in Christ and Church of Independent Word Conventions

Angella Christie, acknowledging God as her source, looks forward to greater exposure in the Christian and secular market, both nationally and internationally. At 5'3" and 118 lbs. she is an awesome sax player - she circular breathes with the best of them – You got to see/hear her to believe it! And, you can hear Angella on her new CD titled *Walk With Me* (AR-1291-2), Artifax Records, 604 Overview Lane, Franklin, TN 37064.

CLARENCE CLEMONS

Clarence Clemons was born on January 11, 1942 in Norfolk, Virginia. He played in **Bruce Springsteen's E Street Band** from 1973 through 1989.

In 1985, he had a #18 hit titled *You're A Friend of Mine* with **Jackson Browne**. Clarence is also well known for his very powerful full toned solo on *Freeway Of Love*, a major hit record by **Aretha Franklin** which reached #3 in 1985.

Photo courtesy Columbia/CBS Records. *"Rescue"* by Clarence Clemons and the Red Bank Rockers

SLAP TONGUE

Although this particular effect is seldom heard, it can be used to enhance certain rhythms while playing with a band. You can readily hear the effect when the band takes a break and only the drum is playing. If the drummer is playing a straight beat the saxophonist can use the slap tongue effect to produce an alternate rhythm over the microphone which can be entertaining and amusing. If you can obtain the 1962 recording of *Night Train* by the **James Brown Band** on King Record #5614, you will hear the effect of the slap tongue being used on the second part of the melody. A musical example can be heard on the tape as we combine this effect with the drums as illustrated;

The slap tongue technique is obtained by suction. The tongue should lay flat against the shaved area of the reed and the lips have to be tightened around the mouthpiece in order to create an air tight seal. You then force the tongue downward and release the air at the same time into the mouthpiece. The combination of this movement as well as the natural sound of the reed will produce the effect. **At this time turn to the instructional tape for an illustration**.

EXAMPLE 13

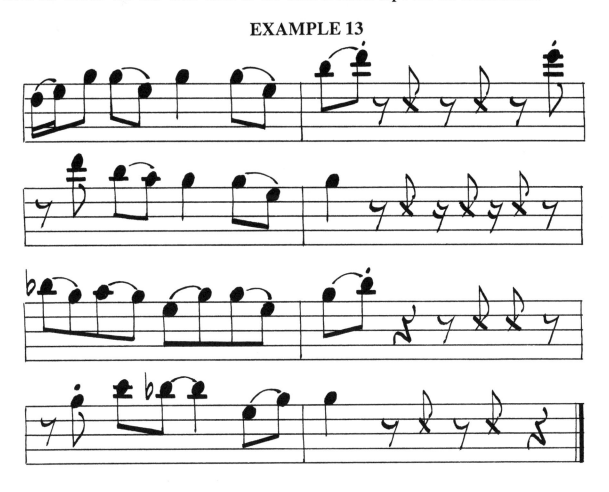

JOHNNY COLLA

A fixture on the San Francisco music scene for twenty years, Johnny Colla played with such artists as **Sly and the Family Stone** and **Van Morrison** before becoming a founding member of **Huey Lewis and the News** in 1979. He is co-author of many of the band's hits, including *Heart of Rock and Roll, If This Is It,* and *Power of Love.*

Johnny uses a Berg Larsen rubber mouthpiece, 125 over 1 and #1 to #4 reeds, depending on the type of music, and his main horn is an old Selmer balanced-action, serial #124,395.

Photographer - Don Kellogg

Huey Lewis and The News

1982	#7	*Do You Believe In Love*
1982	#36	*Hope You Love Me Like You Say You Do*
1983	#8	*Heart and Soul*
1984	#6	*I Want A New Drug*
1984	#6	*The Heart Of Rock & Roll*
1984	#6	*If This Is It*
1984	#18	*Walking On A Thin Line*
1985	#1	*The Power Of Love*
1986	#1	*Stuck With You*
1986	#3	*Hip To Be Square*
1987	#1	*Jacob's Ladder*
1987	#9	*I Know What I Like*
1987	#6	*Doing It All For My Baby*
1988	#3	*Perfect World*
1988	#25	*Small World*
1991	#11	*Couple Days Off*

KING CURTIS

Born Curtis Ousley in Ft. Worth, Texas in 1934. He was inspired to take up saxophone when he heard Louis Jordan on the radio. Curtis began playing alto at age ten and was playing gigs six years later while in high school. At age seventeen, he was leading his own band in Texas clubs. He moved to New York in 1952 and began playing tenor saxophone. King Curtis was one of the most in-demand tenormen for R&B record sessions. He was soon performing 16 record dates a week and made 26 albums under his own name. His biggest break came with *Yakety Yak*, a 1958 #1 hit by the **Coasters**. Curtis' "staccato" tenor solo went around the world. He became affiliated with Atlantic Records from 1958-1959 and 1965-1971. He also led the **Kingpins**, the fantastic accompanying band for **Aretha Franklin**. His solos appear on many albums including hits by **Wilson Pickett** and **The Rascals**. In 1971, King Curtis was stabbed to death outside a Manhattan brownstone he owned when he told a loiterer to move on. He was thirty-seven years old.

Photo courtesy
ATLANTIC RECORDS
"Atlantic Honkers" #8166-1
A Rhythm & Blues
Saxophone Anthology

KING CURTIS

GREATEST HITS

MEMPHIS • WATERMELON MAN • TANYA •
MY LAST DATE WITH YOU

Photo courtesy EVERGREEN RECORDS
#269053 "Greatest Hits"

Solo hits include;

1962	#17	*Soul Twist*
1964	#51	*Soul Serenade*
1967	#33	*Memphis Soul Stew*
1967	#28	*Ode to Billie Joe*
1971	#64	*Whole Lotta Love*

NOTE BENDING and SLIDING

Note bending is one of the oldest forms of altering a note and has been used for many years in blues. Instruments which can be adjusted by embouchure movement or by bending strings, such as a guitar, can use this technique. One of the most popular instruments for this purpose is the blues harmonica. Although it is not strictly related to blues, the technique of note bending tends to be identified with this form of music.

One of the classic hits which featured this technique was *What Does It Take (To Win Your Love)* by **Jr. Walker and The All Stars** (1969 - Soul 35062). **Jr. Walker** began the solo with an introductory altissimo note then, using the lip bend, let the note drop to the upper register of the tenor.

Another excellent example is heard in the tenor solo of *I'm Not In Love* by **Will To Power** (1990 - EPIC 34T 73636). In measure 11, the tenor plays an altissimo note and bends the note downward for the conclusion of this super solo.

Note sliding, also called **glissando**, can be associated with the technique used on the trombone when the slide goes from first position all the way out to seventh position letting the pitch drop as the slide is extended. This can also be done in reverse.

In the 1991 hit *Unforgettable* by **Natalie Cole** with **Nat "King" Cole** (Elektra 94-64875), the tenor solo includes an excellent glissando, or slide effect between measure 8 and measure 9 for the end of the solo. Another great example is *Everything* by **Jody Watley** (1989 MCA 53714). The tenor plays a quick glissando from the low register all the way into the altissimo range!

Note bending is done by the adjustment of the pressure of the lower lip and jaw. Our first step in learning to bend a note is to play a third space C and move your lower jaw up and down while producing a tone. The more the jaw is lowered and raised the more the note will be altered. Incidentally, this could also be used as a lesson in the art of "vibrato" which is the topic of Lesson Nine.

At this time please refer to the study guide tape for the lesson in note bending.

EXAMPLE 14

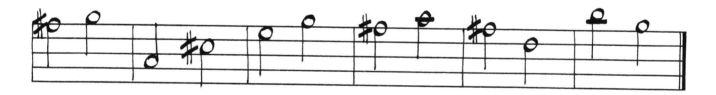

The next step is the process of sliding. This can be done over a range of several notes to a complete octave or more as heard in the following example.

EXAMPLE 15

Whether dealing with **bending** or **sliding** from one pitch to another, you must realize that the most important factor is the looseness of the lower lip and jaw in order to obtain control.

One of the difficulties involved in learning this concept is the fact that we are taught to use a firm embouchure in the early years of our training which is the correct way to support a classical tone. This lesson simply contradicts that approach. You should realize that this is only another means of musical expression and you should use this only in the style in which it is intended.

Please refer to the study guide tape for the effect of note sliding.

EXAMPLE 16

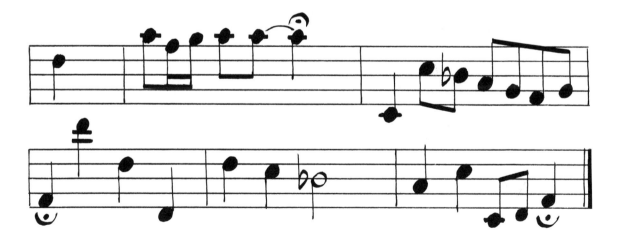

Steve Douglas

STEVE DOUGLAS has been an integral part of the popular music scene from the dawning of rock'n'roll in the Fifties to the current sophisticated sounds of the nineties. Along the way he has amassed an awesome list of credentials as a sax and flute soloist, composer, producer, arranger and record company executive. His lengthy credits include playing with superstars from Elvis Presley to Bob Dylan as well as developing long term working relationships with Phil Spector, Brian Wilson & The Beach Boys, and Ry Cooder.

In between being one of the most in-demand players for both studio sessions and touring, Douglas also has found time to record a dozen solo albums over the years. His latest solo project, Beyond Broadway on the EssDee Music Company label, is a contemporary jazz album full of subtle world music influences. "I wanted to share with the listener my impressions of some exotic countries around the world that I spent time in," he says. "The idea is that this music goes a step beyond Broadway, which symbolizes pop culture and mainstream music."

Douglas' trademark saxophone sound was first developed on early rock'n'roll, R&B and blues recordings. As a teenager growing up in Los Angeles in the Fifties, Steve got to play concerts backing up artists such as Ritchie Valens, Johnny Guitar Watson, Thurston Harris, Don & Dewey, The Sharps (later The Rivingtons), and many others. "Many times I was the only white guy on the bandstand, and I thought that was really cool."

Right after graduating from high school, Douglas joined instrumental guitarist Duane Eddy and The Rebels to record two albums and tour extensively. Steve played the sax solos on such hits as "Forty Miles of Bad Road," "Peter Gunn," "Yep!" and "Cannonball." They were notorius for being the second white group to ever play Harlem's famed Apollo Theater and for being one of the loudest groups at the time with custom-made amplifiers. Right after leaving Eddy, Douglas recorded his own first two albums for Crown Records. "I wrote, arranged, produced, played on and sang the songs. The record company gave me two-hundred bucks."

Steve suddenly found himself in demand as a session player, especially after he reconnected with former high-school mate Phil Spector. Douglas played on some early Crystals records in New York. Then Spector called and asked him to put together the best studio band he could find in Los Angeles. They became known as both "The Wrecking Crew" and "The Wall of Sound Band." Steve played on hit after hit that Spector produced -- the Crystals' "He's a Rebel," "Da Doo Ron Ron" and "Then He Kissed Me"; the Ronettes' "Be My Baby"; and Darlene Love's "(Today I Met) The Boy I'm Gonna Marry." All of the sax solos on the Spector classics from that era were by Douglas.

About that time Brian Wilson called Steve and asked him if he could put together a band like Spector's for some sessions by The Beach Boys. Douglas' association started with "Surfin' U.S.A." and included virtually all of The Beach Boys' biggest hits through "Good Vibrations" and then again later on albums such as 15 Big Ones.

"All of a sudden," remembers Douglas, "the West Coast music scene exploded." Steve became popular with all of the surfing and hot rod recording groups; and he recorded with Jan & Dean, Dick Dale, Bruce (Johnston) & Terry (Melcher), Gary Usher, The Ventures, Richard Delvey & The Challengers, and others. Douglas also led his own recording groups in this genre including The Catalinas (known for a Douglas-penned tune, "Bonzai Washout"), the Custom Kings, The Vets and the Liberation Street Band. During this period Douglas also recorded with many R&B artists including B.B. King (a half-dozen albums) and Bob & Earl ("Harlen Shuffle").

Douglas worked with Elvis Presley, first to portray one of The King's band members in the film "Girls Girls Girls" (the band recorded "Return to Sender" live on camera), and then in the studio to record a double-sided hit for another movie ("Viva Las Vegas"/"What'd I Say").

In the mid-Sixties, Steve worked for Bobby Darin's TM Music publishing company and then moved on to Capitol Records as a staff producer and A&R executive. He produced an impressive string of hits including Glen Campbell's "The Universal Soldier," Wayne Newton's "Danke Schoen," The Lettermen's "Theme From 'A Summer Place'" and, Billy Preston's Top 5 R&B album Wildest Organ in Town. Douglas switched to Mercury Records runing the West Coast office and signed artists like Leon Russell and Blue Cheer. Steve recorded his own album for Mercury, Reflections of a Golden Horn. He started his own label, Pentagram Records, with engineering ace Al Schmitt; bought a Hollywood studio; and put out albums by Big Mama Thornton and Redeye (who had a Top 30 hit, "Games").

In 1976, Steve went to Egypt and became the first musician to record inside the King's Chamber of the Great Pyramid. The resulting album, The Music of Cehops, became a best seller primarily through mail-order and alternative retail outlets.

Steve relocated to the San Francisco Bay Area performing and recording with numerous top acts including Steve Perry (Street Talk album), the Tubes, John Greg Kihn, Sammy Hagar and The Replacements.

Douglas can be heard playing on the soundtracks of such movies as "Fast Times at Ridgemont High," "American Hot Wax," "Streets of Fire," "Gremlins," "Top Gun," "Brewster's Millions," "The Blues Brothers" and many others. He also has performed on the scores for numerous popular TV shows including "Moonlighting" and "Twilight Zone."

In the early Eighties, Steve recorded a jazz album, Rainbow Suite, which received only limited distribution. But he soon signed with Fantasy Records and recorded two more jazz recordings -- the all-digital live Hot Sax (which went to #3 on Radio & Records' national jazz airplay chart) and King Kobra (which included a duet with Ry Cooder).

Douglas also has learned to play keyboards, synthesizers and computers to broaden his abilities in creating his own music. After being mesmerized by a 28-piece gamalon orchestra while traveling in Bali, he returned there last year and digitally recorded many of the instruments of the region so that he could sample them at his own studio and incorporate them into his arrangements of his original compositions. "I love the flavor those sounds can add. Many of their instruments are manufactured in pairs to be played together and one instrument is slightly out-of-tune with the other." With his new Beyond Broadway album, Douglas says, "I wanted to share my feelings and impressions from many of the places I've traveled, especially Bali."

The album contains musical influences from Bali ("Balinese Rhapsody," "Trip to Market" and "Journey To Shangri-La"), Spain ("Spanish Nights"), Central America ("Reflections at Xel-Ha," an inspirational limestone lagoon and Mayan ruin in Yucatan), India ("Etched in India") and Java ("Java Jive").

"I've come to a place in my life where the only musical world I have left to conquer is my own music. I've been seduced again and again by the rich life of playing sessions or tours. But for now I only want to record my own music and play with my own band. That's the ultimate satisfaction."

STEVE DOUGLAS EQUIPMENT LIST

Selmer Mark VI Baritrone Sax	Selmer Mark VI French Made Alto Sax
King Super 20 Tenor Sax	Grafton Plastic Alto Sax
Buescher Straight Alto Sax	Buffett Soprano Sax
Haynes C Flute	Artley Bass Flute
Artley Piccolo	

I have a large collection of flutes, recorders, ocarinas and other native flutes from around the world.

I use Rico Plasticover reeds on all saxes.

The "First Saxman"

President Bill Clinton with shades on playing his Selmer tenor on the Arsenio Hall TV show, the song? "Heart Break Hotel".

PRESIDENTIAL TENOR SAXOPHONE
LIMITED EDITION
SERIES OF 150 PIECES TO BE BUILT IN 1993

#1 of 150 was presented to President Bill Clinton and in turn/time dedicated to the Shrine to Music Museum in Vermillion, South Dakota.

Richard Elliot is playing #2 of 150 on his latest tour supporting the new album *Soul Embrace* on Manhattan Records.

L. A. SAX COMPANY a division of BARRINGTON MUSIC PRODUCTS Inc.
22N159 Pepper Road • Barrington, IL 60010

President Pete LaPlaca
Director of Artist Relations H. Allan

RICHARD ELLIOT

From the pulsating rhythms of "Sweat," the opening track, all the way to the dark, moody beauty of "Alone at Sea," one thing's patently clear: with **Soul Embrace**, his second album for Capitol/Manhattan records, multi-talented sax man **Richard Elliot** has created a record that truly showcases the dynamic range of his talent and artistry.

"I wanted to cover a wide gamut of music without losing any continuity," says Elliot, whose popularity has been growing steadily since the release of his first solo album in 1984. "And to make sure that I covered a musical range, 25 songs were recorded. I pared it down to 15, and then it was tough deciding what to leave out. We ultimately kept all 15 on the record. Hopefully, in this day and age, that means we're giving people value for money!"

Elliot need have no fear: Soul Embrace is jam-packed with some of the strongest material he's ever cut. Aside from an emotive reading of the 10CC classic "I'm Not in love," Elliot originals such as the warm, melodic "Heartland" and "Calle del Soul," a bright and breezy track ("inspired by local musicians in Puerto Rico"), reveal Elliot's ongoing desire to expand his creative horizons. "On previous albums, my performances have sometimes been very hard-hitting. I felt that I had to bear down to really convey emotion and feeling," says Elliot, who wrote 10 and produced 12 songs on the album. "This time, I used a more delicate approach on some of the material. I wanted to try and convey the same emotional intensity by using subtlety. I feel that tracks like 'Because I Love You' and 'Sweet Dream' really express that side of me."

Emphasizing his long-held passion for R&B and urban music, Elliot has also included three tracks featuring different vocalists. The album features sterling performances by Capitol label mates D'Atra Hicks ("Promises") and Gary Brown ("Lost in a Minute") and newcomer Fred Johnson ("Never Gonna Break Your Heart"). Johnson has been a featured singer with Elliot's busy touring band for the past eight months. He notes, "I like to do vocal tunes because they give me the opportunity to broaden my audience -- and I'm not shy about that!"

Scottish-born Elliot (who grew up in Los Angeles) remembers trying the accordion before settling on the saxophone at summer school. "I wanted to take up another instrument and the sax looked cool...I liked the shape of it," he recalls, and after showing his obvious aptitude for the instrument, Elliot was encouraged by his high school music director (also a working studio musician) to pursue a musical career.

After landing an audition for a summer job touring the Far East with Natalie Cole and The Pointer Sisters, Elliot returned to the U.S. and spent two years with the trend-setting fusion group Kittyhawk, recording three albums (two for EMI and one for Zebra/MCA), in the process honing his skills in the studio.

After completing tours with Kittyhawk, Elliot toured with Rickie Lee Jones before joining The Yellowjackets to work on their second Warner Brothers album. When the group took a one-year hiatus, Elliot was quickly snapped up by singer/songwriter Melissa Manchester for her band, occasionally filling in for a friend on gigs with the legendary Tower of Power.

In 1982, the group offered Elliot a permanent place in its auspicious line-up: "I think being with Tower of Power helped me grow as a musician, as a performer and as a team player. I grew and developed more with that group than with any other band I've ever worked with."

Photo: Karen Kuehn 1993

In 1987, after five years with Tower of Power and with the release date of his third solo album approaching, Elliot felt he was ready to fully commit to his solo career and began the process of building an audience for himself nationwide. Through a series of five albums (Initial Approach, Trolltown, The Power of Suggestion, Take It To The Skies, and What's Inside) initially released on Enigma Records and reissued by Capitol/Manhattan Records in 1991, Elliot's sure but steady approach to creating a following for his music began to pay off.

With the September, 91 release of On The Town, his Capitol/Manhattan Records debut, Elliot began to see tangible results with a strong chart showing and his best year ever. Containing key tracks like "Into the Light," "Stiletto Heels," the infectious title cut and "Take This Heart" (featuring vocalist Carl Anderson), On The Town logged several weeks topping the nation's contemporary jazz radio charts, further establishing him as a key recording artist and performer.

Now comes Soul Embrace, a collection of material that promises to take Richard Elliot to a new level of recognition and acclaim. With musicians Craig Yamek, Ron Reinhardt, Naoki Yanai and Richard Smith. Elliot has forged an album that exudes energy, spirit and vitality. "We do about 100 dates together, so no one's going to have a better idea of interpreting music than the guys I share the stage with."

He credits his wife, Michele, for suggesting he record "I'm Not in Love," a pop classic that he says "lent itself to instrumental interpretation once I started trying it out. Originally, I didn't think it would work and I tried it with the tenor sax. Somehow that didn't feel right so it's the only tune on the album where I'm playing soprano sax, and I think we've captured the mood of the original playing while giving the song a more current sound."

Whether tapping into straight-up '90s street grooves with "Lost in a Minute" via drum loops provided by a team known as "Red 326," hitting hard with the strong R&B flavor of "Promises" or expressing himself with warmth and sensitivity on "By the Fire," Richard Elliot is forging new musical pathways for himself, captivating music lovers with his Soul Embrace on Manhattan CD #98946.

Photo and biography courtesy **L.A.SAX**. According to L.A. SAX, Richard Elliot is the "Eddie Van Halen of sax players."

Richard Elliot Composer/Arranger/Saxophonist

Personal Management: Matt Kramer, P. O. Box 543, Santa Monica, CA 90406

TELEVISION:
ARSENIO HALL SHOW - Guest artist
VH-1 - Featured live performances and music videos
BET - Music videos, Ramsey Lewis Show
SNIFF - Title theme, underscore (New World Pictures/CBS)
COVER-UP '88 - Documentary-title theme, underscore (Empowerment Project)
DAVID LETTERMAN - live appearance (NBX)
SOLID GOLD - live appearance
A YEAR IN THE LIFE - featured player (NBC)
PRIVATE EYE - featured player (Universal)
SIMON & SIMON - featured player (CBS)
VERONICA CLARE - featured player (Lifetime)

FILM:
TEENWITCH - Underscore-composed and performed (Transworld)
DREAM TEAM - Featured artist (Universal)
THREE FUGITIVES - Featured artist (Touchstone)
WIRED - Featured artist, actor (Atlantic Films)
TOP GUN - Source music (Paramount)
ONE MORE SATURDAY NIGHT - Featured artist - title, underscore (Columbia)
TWICE UPON A TIME - Title Theme (LADD)

COMMERCIALS:
GENERAL ELECTRIC - composed, produced
FOX TV - composed, produced
MICHELOB - (with Etta James) - featured artist
MCDONALD'S - featured artist
DODGE - actor

ALBUMS: (recorded)

Huey Lewis & The News	The Temptations
Smokey Robinson	Stacy Lattisaw
Michael McDonald	Tiffany
Manhattan Transfer	Deniece Williams
Tower Of Power	The Four Tops
The Yellowjackets	

LIFE PERFORMANCES:

Huey Lewis & The News	
Manhattan Transfer	Tower of Power
Rickie Lee Jones	Robert Cray
Natalie Cole	The Pointer Sisters
Melissa Manchester	Alphonse Mouzon
	The Yellowjackets

SOLO ALBUMS: (produced)
SOUL EMBRACE (1993) - Richard Elliot - Manhattan Records (#1 on Billboard Top
Contemporary Jazz Albums - 4/93 and #1 on NAC National Airplay - 3/93)
ON THE TOWN (1991) - Richard Elliot - Manhattan Records
WHAT'S INSIDE (1990) - Richard Elliot - Enigma Records
TAKE TO THE SKIES (1989) - Richard Elliot - Intima/Enigma Records
POWER OF SUGGESTION (1988) - Richard Elliot - Intima/Enigma Records
TROLLTOWN (1986) - Richard Elliot - Intima/Enigma Records
INITIAL APPROACH (1984) - Richard Elliot - Intima/Enigma Records
ISN'T IT AMAZING (1989) - Robin & Micheal Goodrow - Amazing Records

TRILL

Every student involved in classroom music will have played a trill at one time or another. The trill is very popular in many forms of music and represents yet another technique for producing an effect which can be utilized to enhance solo performances.

The trill, as reviewed in this study, pertains primarily to the concept of rock and roll and blues style playing. Trills can be utilized by using the base note and trilling to a step higher or lower. For example, if you play a G above the staff and move the F key back and forth you will produce a trill from G to F or F to G. By playing the same G and utilizing both F and E you will continue to produce a trill involving more than one step. The speed of a trill will depend upon the type of effect that you want to produce. It may be a slow waver or a rapid movement as demonstrated on the study tape.

EXAMPLE 17

EXAMPLE 18   SOLO ILLUSTRATION

A trill within a progression of steps is very popular. The illustration used will move from high B to C to C sharp then to high D. While you begin on B and continue up to D, the trilling effect is utilized by pressing the high F key under the right hand on the side of the saxophone.

Please refer to the cassette.

EXAMPLE 19

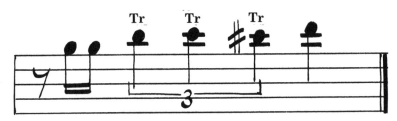

Other examples of a trill performed on tenor saxophone are illustrated in the 1988 hit, *Get Outta My Dreams, Get Into My Car* by **Billy Ocean**, the 1992 hit, *Love Is A Wonderful Thing* by **Michael Bolton** and *Heart On The Line* by **Richard Marx**.
There are many combinations of trills which can be utilized. It is simply a matter of determining which combination of notes you want to use for a particular solo. You will need to learn alternate fingerings in many cases in order to utilize the trill. A fingering chart will show the various combinations of notes and alternate fingerings for those notes. Some "alternate notes" would not normally be played as half or whole notes because the tone may not be very good, however you can use them for the purpose of the trill due to the speed that is involved.

KENNY G
"A Master of Beautiful Melodies"

Kenny G is from Seattle, Washington. When he was ten years old, he heard someone play saxophone on T.V. on the **Ed Sullivan Show**. His mother rented him a horn and no one ever had to tell him to practice. Early inspirations include **Grover Washington, Stanley Turrentine, Ronnie Laws, David Sanborn** and **Michael Brecker**. Kenny G's style was largely influenced by R&B. While in high school, he played in the school's big band and at age seventeen was asked to play with **Barry White's Love Unlimited Orchestra**. He practiced four hours a day for a dozen years. He graduated at the University of Washington. While studying accounting during the day he played gigs at night and joined the University Jazz band. At age twenty, he joined **Jeff Lorber's** band for five years. He soon recorded his first album and the rest is history. His unique soprano sax tone is a trademark. During a live performance, Kenny G's personality is a hit and his stage presence is hypnotic. He concludes his concerts by walking among an enthusiastic audience while ad libing through his wireless microphone. Occasionally he shakes someone's hand and appears to be smiling all the time. He is a true entertainer. And Kenny G is the biggest-selling instrumental artist in the history of his genre. Collectively he has sold over 10 million records with all his releases!

Major hits include;

Year	Chart	Title
1987	#4	*Songbird*
1987	#15	*Don't Make Me Wait For Love*
1988	#13	*Silhouette*
1989		*Going Home*
1992	#1	*Forever In Love*

Albums:

Kenny G	*Duotones*
G-Force	*Gravity*
Silhouette	*Kenny G Live*
Breathless	

LITTLE RICHARD and GRADY GAINES
(circa 1955)

Grady Gaines is the only human ever to upstage the architect of Rock 'n' Roll, **Little Richard**. During the 1950's he was the band leader of the **Upsetters**. Grady would jump on top of Little Richard's baby grand and blow a pulverizing solo. Grady also performed with **Johnny Ace, "Gatemouth" Brown, Bobby "Blue" Bland, Dee Clark, Little Willie John, James Brown, Sam Cooke, Jackie Wilson, Joe Tex** and **Lee Diamond**.

Photo courtesy **Black-Top Records - A. Hammond Scott**, Box 56691, New Orleans, LA 70156.

From the album *Full Gain* by **Grady Gaines and the Texas Upsetters**. Record #BT-1041.

VIBRATO

I referred to vibrato in chapter seven when the effect of note bending was reviewed. For saxophone we will use the approach of the lower jaw movement in order to produce a vibrato.

There are three basic methods of obtaining a vibrato on a wind instrument. One method is diaphragm vibrato. The performer produces impulses of wind across the tone hole. This method is used by flutists.

Another method of vibrato is produced by the movement of the hand over the keys such as a trumpet. You will note that the trombone can achieve this effect by moving the slide back and forth from a half inch to an inch and a half depending upon the width of the vibrato.

The third technique of vibrato is produced by moving the lower jaw up and down. This is the concept that we will use for saxophone. The beginning stage of vibrato can be done by using only the mouthpiece and the neck of the saxophone to produce a tone while moving the lower jaw up and down which causes the tone to waver. The lower or higher the jaw is moved, the wider the vibrato. It will be up to you to determine the desired width and speed. Once you have worked with the mouthpiece and the neck for a while, you should assemble the instrument and play third space C and continue the movement of the jaw and work toward a steady "waver".

Please refer to the tape at this time.

EXAMPLE 20

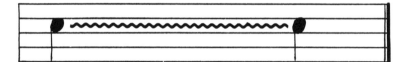

EXAMPLE 21

During the process of learning the vibrato, you will become aware of various styles while listening to music on the radio or watching television. You will soon realize that there are just as many styles of vibrato as there are music.

For example, during the big band swing era of the 1930's and 40's, a wide rapid vibrato was in style. Some of the soloists in the 1950's and 60's continued to use a rapid vibrato, especially at the very end of a note. As pop music evolved, the vibrato became slower and not as wide.

HERBERT HARDESTY

Herbert Hardesty was born March 3, 1925 in New Orleans, LA. His music studies began at an early age at school, private lessons and later at Dillard University. Additional training came from the musicians in big bands and small groups performing Be Bop and Jazz along with the Blues and Rock and Roll of the day.

Hardesty has recorded with many artists in cities such as New Orleans, New York and California. He began his first U.S. tour with **Roy Brown**, a famous New Orleans Blues singer who had many hits including *Good Rockin' Tonight*. He returned to New Orleans and continued to work with big bands which demanded excellent readers to handle the sight reading. After two years, Herbert decided to form his own band and, as a result of his reading ability and distinctive solo style, he was called to work in local recording studios with many new artists, including **Lloyd Price**. His tenor solo was featured on Prices' *Laudy Miss Claudy*.

However, it is through the Top 40 hits by **Fats Domino** that many saxophonists know the upbeat "good feelin" solo style made famous by Herbert Hardesty. His solos were heard on juke boxes and airways all over the world in the following hits;

1955	#10	*Ain't That A Shame*
1959	#17	*I'm Gonna Be A Wheel Someday*
1959	#19	*My Blue Heaven*
1961	#15	*Let The Four Winds Blow*
1959	#50	*Saints Go Marching In*
1956	#14	*When My Dreamboat Comes Home*
1957	#4	*I'm Walking*
1957	#5	*Blue Monday*

Hardesty continues to appear as a guest soloist on many albums. He recently recorded with **Al Hirt** and **Pete Fountain**. He also appears on a 1992 recording by **Dr. Jones** and is due to perform on a future recording by the legendary **Count Basie Big Band**. And, he continues to travel with **Fats Domino** throughout the world.

Herbert Hardesty plays a Selmer Mark VI and a Super Action 80 which was presented to him by Selmer during a concert in Paris. He uses an Otto Link #10 mouthpiece and Rico Royal #3 and La Voz medium reeds. Asked about his approach to performance, Herb Hardesty states, "I believe in good tone and never to over blow the horn."

JOHNNY & THE HURRICANES

Saxophonist Johnny Paris was born in Walbridge near Toledo, Ohio in 1940. Johnny was inspired by **Rudy Pompilli**, saxophonist with **Bill Haley and The Comets**, and **Sil Austin** who were creating Top 40 hits. In 1959 the band recorded *Crossfire* which reached #23 on the Top 40 charts. Personnel included Johnny Paris (tenor saxophone), Paul Tesluk (Hammond organ), Dave Yorko (guitar), Butch Mattice (bass) and Tony Kaye (drums). Their lively reverb sound was obtained by letting the music bounce around in the large auditorium of Detroit's Carmen Towers. Hits included;

1959	#23	*Crossfire*
1959	#5	*Red River Rock*
1959	#25	*Reveille Rock*
1960	#15	*Beatnik Fly*
1960	#48	*Down Yonder*
1960	#97	*Revival*
1960	#60	*Rocking Goose*
1961	#86	*Ja-Da*

Photo courtesy Victor Records - VIP - 4027 *"Best of Johnny & The Hurricanes"*

SUBTONE

The saxophone has the potential to produce many different tones in the low register. The most common tone is one which I refer to as the "open" or "classical" tone. For excellent examples of the classical tone, you should listen to recordings by artists such as **David Bilger, Paul Brodie, Neal Ramsay** and **Sigurd Rascher**. For a complete CD list write to *Woodwind Services, Box 206, Medfield, MA 02052.*

The "subtone" on the other hand, is a method by which the artist can render a softer tone in the low register. It is sometimes referred to as an "airy sound".

EXAMPLE 22

The technique of the subtone is generally not associated with rock and roll, however, it has been my experience that many of the ballads performed through the years in rock and roll and pop music called for a saxophonist to play in the low register utilizing the subtone approach. A classic example of this type of ballad performance can be heard on *Plays Pretty For The People* by **Sil Austin** on PolyGram 832351.

The subtone is a technique which can be very difficult to master. The process of setting the embouchure to obtain a subtone is totally contradictory to the embouchure used to produce the traditional saxophone tone in the low register. The performer will need to roll (draw back) most of the lower lip inside the mouth. In order to produce the effect of the subtone, one does not utilize the stretched and thin bottom lip. The subtone calls for a very loose lower lip with the majority of the skin touching a large amount of the reed.

EXAMPLE 23

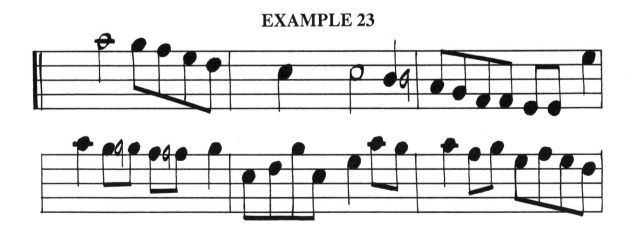

The following pictures
illustrate the difference between the embouchures.

These photographs illustrate the thin stretched mouth.
Please note that the sides are drawn back and up.

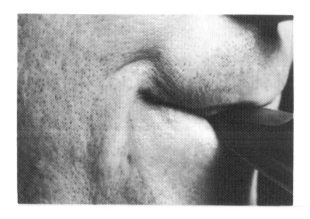 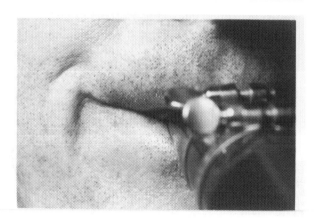

These photographs show a more relaxed
embouchure for the subtone technique.
<u>Also note that there is more mouthpiece</u>
<u>inside the mouth for subtone purposes.</u>

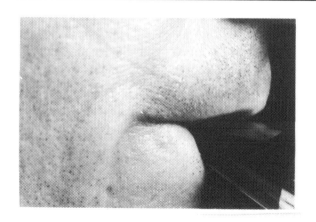 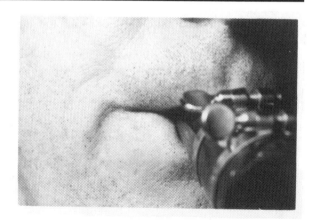

DAVE KOZ

Contemporary sax player **Dave Koz** has a natural skill for expressing classic pop melodies and jazz stylings that explode with a wonderfully contagious spirit. Not only is he a genuine master of his instrument, he also happens to be one of the nicest guys you're ever likely to meet. From his first gigs in high school to prostints with Bobby Caldwell, Jeff Lorber, Tom Scott, Richard Marx and countless others, it was only a matter of time before Koz's spectacular pop saxophone was to grace an album of his own. The impressive range of his scope – with an easy flair for pop, jazz and R&B – is beautifully expressed on **Dave Koz**, his debut album on Capitol Records. For good reason, the Top 10 A/C hit single **Castle of Dreams** scaled the New Adult Contemporary chart to the #1 spot. After just one listen to Dave's engaging style, it's easy to understand why music fans and critics alike are joining the Koz.

Although still in his 20s, Dave has already made an impressive mark on the recording industry as one of the most in-demand session players around. He's played on albums for everyone from Tom Scott to Joan Armatrading, Natalie Cole to Gladys Knight & The Pips, the Commodores to U2 on the huge bluesy re-mix of "When Love Comes To Town." He has quickly earned the respect of his peers in the business, both as a consummate studio player and a showstopping live performer. Now he's ready to show the world.

Dave Koz is a masterful introduction. Koz's first single -- the delightful Top 10 "Castle of Dreams" -- became the first breakthrough A/C track of 1991, and continued to gain ground with an exotic video filmed in Italy. It's streak to #1 on the New Adult Contemporary chart (Radio & Records January 25, 1991), surpassed such stellar artists as Joe Sample, Paul Simon and George Michael.

Dave was born in L.A.'s San Fernando Valley, and first took to the saxophone in Junior High School, encouraged by his brother Jeff, now a noted commercial composer. "I picked it up and it felt totally natural" he says now. "I got half way decent enough to pick up jobs by the age of 15."

Dave studied jazz while in high school, just after graduating from UCLA, he got the call to play with Bobby Caldwell. "It was an incredible band. I owe a lot to him for giving me a shot and getting the ball rolling." Soon he was playing with Jeff Lorber, a connection that, to hear Dave tell it, "has turned into a great relationship that is still very, very strong. It was a great thrill to meet Jeff" Dave remembers. "He was a big part of my musical upbringing, so when I got to audition for him, I just freaked out."

"His house was an unbelievable place -- the studio had something like 400 synthesizers in it and no room to even walk. I started jamming on something and he said, 'OK, you've got the gig.' I couldn't believe it! We toured for about three months, culminating with the Playboy Jazz Festival. It was wild. I had a wireless mike and ran out into the audience and up and down the Hollywood Bowl. It was one of those special moments in my life." Lorber seconded the emotion by producing three tracks on Dave's debut.

The combination of doing a jazz/R&B tour with Lorber and a rock tour with Richard Marx in front of thousands of people the world over was "an amazing experience," Dave says. "It pushed me so much. I love to entertain and, fortunately, I was lucky enough to work with people that allowed me to do that. Richard wanted to have a show that was really exciting and fun to be a part of. He welcomed that kind of input from everybody." Dave wrote a song with him for Dave Koz, and also cut an instrumental version of "Endless Summer Nights," one of Marx's biggest hits.

His recent exploits have ranged from Donny Osmond's comeback albums and accompanying acclaimed new singer/songwriter Hugh Harris in concert, to soundtrack work on television and the theme song for Three Men And A Little Lady. With his own band, Dave is embarking on his first headlining U.S. dates. "I'm looking forward to this tour more than any other. I want to see people's faces when they hear this music live. Playing live is probably the best part of it all for me. When the horn is in my mouth, that's the easy part. It's definitely going to push me into a situation I've never been in before and that already makes it a positive experience for me."

Dave's enthusiasm is equally infectious on stage and off. He has the gifted quality of combining youthful reverence with a rare and timeless musical instinct. His pop influences include Sting, Peter Gabriel and Luther Vandross as well as composers Quincy Jones and Dave Grusin while he shares an admiration for other young saxophone players like Kirk Whalum and Gerald Albright.

"The making of this record turned out to be totally different than I expected it to be," Dave admits. "I learned a lot in each relationship I had with the album's various producers. It's hard for that stuff not to rub off. It was a great thrill to be working with people that I respected so much. I really couldn't ask for a better experience on my first record."

Koz's Additional Sessions

Joan Armatrading, Hearts & Flowers
Big Noise, Bang!
Boys Club, Boys Club
Brother Beyond, Trust
Natalie Cole, Good To Be Back
The Commodores, United
Five Star, Rock The World
Good Question, Good Question
Russell Hitchcock, Russell Hitchcock
Thelma Houston, Throw You Down
Jackie Jackson, Be The One
Gladys Knight & The Pips, All Our Love
Richard Marx, Repeat Offender
Donny Osmond, Eyes Don't Lie
George Pettus, George Pettus
The Rippingtons, Kilimanjaro, Moonlighting

Brenda Russell, Get Here
Tom Scott, Them Changes
Soundtrack, Golden Child
Soundtrack, Action Jackson
Soundtrack, Three Men And A Little Lady
U2, "When Love Comes To Town"

...and coming up...

Bobby Caldwell, Hugh Harris,
Jon Lucien, NYC, Phil Perry,
Jonathan Robbins, Jermaine
Stewart, The Temptations,
John Tesh, Shanice Williams

TELEVISON AND FILM PROJECTS

Into The Night/ABC (National) • E! The Inside Word (Cable) • Tonight Show/NBC • Studio 22/CBS • CNN Showbiz Today • Morning Magazine/WGPR • Byron Allen Show/NBC • Home Show/ABC • Studio 59/ABC • Arsenio Hall Show • BET ran Dave & Phil's Live at the Strand • VH-1 Soul of VH-1 Christmas Show • VH-1 Christmas Show • United Cerebral Palsy Telethon • VH-1 Hits Show • Easter Seals Telethon • New York at Night • General Hospital Dave's acting debut+performance • CBS THIS MORNING • REGIS AND CATHY LEE • Lincoln Memorial Sax Jam performance for Bill Clinton, aired live on HBO • Entertainment This Week • Family Matters ABC Network, Dave appeared in acting role as self

* General Hospital has been playing "Emily" as a love theme for the couple Ned and Jenny at least 2-3 times a week since October 1991.
* TV commercial for Arsenio Hall Show aired nationally, the first quarter of 1992.
* TV spot for KTWV aired locally in L.A., the first quarter of 1992.
* Co-wrote, (with Jeff Koz and Audrey Koz), title theme for the NBC comedy series Walter & Emily, plus end credits and all cues.
* Featured instrumentalist on the soundtrack for the film Folks starring Tom Selleck, released May 1, 1992.
* Featured instrumentalist for the new Edward James Olmos film, American Me. Score by Claude Gaudett and Dennis Lambert. Released March 13, 1992.
* March 1993 General Hospital debuts their first new theme song in 30 years! Title and end credits co-written by Dave and Jeff Koz.

AWARDS
Nominated, Best New Age Contemporary Jazz Instrumentalist - Pollstar
Winner, Best Jazz Album - 1st annual Pro Set L.A. Music Awards
CHARTS
"Lucky Man" for eight weeks - #1 NAC Album of 1993
#1 New Adult Contemporary (NAC) for five weeks in a row - R&R
#2 New Adult Contemporary (NAC) Album of the year 1991 - R&R
Top 5 Contemporary Jazz Album - Billboard
#8 Contemporary Jazz Album of the year - Billboard
Top 10 Adult Contemporary (A/C) single "Castle of Dreams" - R&R
#15 Adult Contemporary A/C single of the year "Castle of Dreams" - R&R
Top 10 Adult Contemporary A/C single "Nothing But The Radio On"
#1 single "Emily" in the Philippines, Malaysia, and Hong Kong
LP is Platinum in Malaysia dn Gold in Singapore

EQUIPMENT

	MAKE	M/P	REEDS
Soprano	Yamaha Silver Plated YSS-62	Couf Plastic #8	Rico Plasticover #3 - 3/12
Alto	Yamaha Silver Plated YAS-62	Beechler Metal #7	Rico Plasticover #4
Tenor	Yamaha Custom Silver Plated	Berg Larsen Hard Rubber	Rico Plasticover # 3 1/2
Baritone	Yamaha Y-62	Berg Larsen	Rico Plasticover #4
Microphone	AKG C409, Samson UHF wireless unit		

Photo: Eugene Pinkowski, Photo Courtesy:
VISION MANAGEMENT, 7958 Beverly Blvd., Los Angeles, CA 90048

54

AMY LEE

Saxophonist Amy Lee obtained her Bachelor of Music in jazz performance and music merchandising from the University of Miami, Florida. She has been a member of many performing groups, demonstrating a wide range of musical styles from traditional/avant'garde jazz, R&B/funk and 20th Century classical to alternative dance music. Ms. Lee has performed with many well-known artists including her long stints with *Jimmy Buffett* and *Charles Neville* as well as performances with *Joni Mitchell, James Taylor, Ringo Starr, Ben E. King,* the *Temptations, Clarence "Gatemouth" Brown, Clint Black, Glenn Frey* and the *Atlanta Symphony Orchestra.*

Amy Lee recently finished the *RECESSION RECESS* tour as soloist/horn arranger/section leader for *Jimmy Buffett & the Coral Reefer Band.* As a Coral Reefer, Amy appeared on the TONIGHT SHOW starring Johnny Carson, May 5, 1992, performed on SHOWTIME's Hurricane Relief Benefit, September '92; and toured the continental United States in 1991-92 for the *Outpost Tour* as well as the continental U.S. and Hawaii for the *Recession Recess Tour.* Of all these wonderful experiences, the most memorable is when the Coral Reefer Band was invited to perform at the Tennessee Ball for the 42nd Presidential Inauguration. Amy had the great honor of performing along-side President Bill Clinton when he sat in with the Coral Reefers during Buffett's classic hit, *Changes in Attitude Changes in Lattitude.*

Amy has performed regularly at the New Orleans Jazz & Heritage Festival since 1990. Her 1991 Festival appearances were documented by Island Visual Arts who have released a video titled ":Let the Good Times Roll - A Film About The Roots of American Music" (Polygram 1992). In that same year, the JVC Corporation filmed her performance with Diversity and have been running it in syndication on Japanese television.

Amy Lee has worked extensively in the studio, performing on major and independent albums, as well as radio jingles. Her recent album work was for Margaritaville Records, MCS, for a Coral Reefer Band Sampler. The album will contain an instrumental of hers titled SUGARTOWN SHAKEDOWN and is slated to be released in May '93. Other major album credits include Rowdy Records, a division of La'Face Records for the rap group, Ya'll So Stupid, '93 release date; Luther Barnes, A.I.R. Records, '93 release date; and the Grammy-nominated Richard Smallwood Singers, PORTRAIT (Word, Inc., A&M Records, 1990). Amy has also recorded for the following Independent record release: Kodac Harrison, GLAD TO BE LIVE (Corner Records, 1992); Melanie Hammet, I DREAM WILD HORSES (Mogli Music, Ltd., 1992); and Bob Gillespie, STILL FACES (Southeast Records, 1990). As a composer, Amy has had commissions for various avant-garde works in concert situations and accompaniments for dance. Locally in Atlanta and in the Southeast club circuit, Amy Lee can be seen performing saxophones, flute and singing backup vocals with many different groups including the original acoustic rock band Kodac Harrison & Luckie Street. She also performs in a multidimensional, multidisciplinary capacity with MHP & the Jazz Collective.

Currently Performing With
Nationally: Jimmy Buffett & the Coral Reefer Band, Charles Neville & Diversity
Southeast: Kodac Harrison & Luckie Street, MHP & the Jazz Collective

Previously With
Atlanta Symphony Summer Pops Orchestra, Atlanta Contemporary Chamber Ensemble, Temptations, Ben E. King, Carol Channing and Lou's Blues Revue

National Tours
JIMMY BUFFETT & THE CORAL REEFER BAND
'94 Fruitcakes On Tour, '93 Chameleon Caravan Tour
'92 Recession Recess Tour, '91 Outpost Tour

Album Credits
Major: Jimmy Buffett, *FRUITCAKES* - '94 release/MCA
Coral Reefer Band Sampler, LIFE AT MARGARITAVILLE CAFE - MCA RECORDS '93
Ya'll So Stupid - Rowdy Records - La'Face Records - '93
Luther Barnes - A.I.R. Records - '93
Richard Smallwood Singers - PORTRAIT , Word Inc. - A&M Records '90

Independent: *Kodac Harrison, GLAD TO BE LIVE* - Corner Records '92
Melanie Hammet, I DREAM WILD HORSES - Mogli Music, Ltd. '92
Bob Gillespie, STILL FACES - Southeast Records '90

Television
National: *SHOWTIME Hurricane Relief Benefit Concert* - aired September '92 - Coral Reefer Band
The Tonight Show starring Johnny Carson aired May 5, 1992 - Coral Reefer Band
History of Afro American Music - Syndication 1991 - Diversity
International: JVC Corp. Compilation of New Orleans Jazz & Heritage Festival - Japanese Syndication

Major Video
"Let The Good Times Roll - A film About The Roots of American Music" Island Visual Arts -Polygram '92

Jingles
Applebee's Restaurant - *Late Night At Applebee's;Applebee's Combo* - Babbit & Reiman
Cadillac Dealers of the Southeast - *Cadillac Style* - Babbit & Reiman

Benefits & Festivals
Presidential Inaugural Ball - Tennessee Ball - Washington D.C. '93
Hurricane Relief Concert - Joe Robbie Stadium, Miami, FL '92
Don Henley's *Walden Woods Benefit* - Madison Square Garden '91
New Orleans Jazz & Heritage Festivals - MARS Jazz Tent, Fairgrounds '90-'93
Atlanta Arts Festival - Piedmont Pak, Atlanta '91
Mattress Factory - King Plow Arts Center, Atlanta '91
Martin Luther King, Jr. Celebration - Atlanta Civic Center '90
Atlanta Mayor Maynard Jackson's Victory Party '89
National Endowment for the Arts, American Music Week, Atlanta '85-'87

Equipment List

INSTR.	BRAND/MODEL	YR	MOUTHPIECE	LIGATURE	REED
ALTO	YAMAHA-YAS 62	'78	ROVNER DEEP "V" LF METAL-SIZE 9L	ROVNER GRADIENT LM	LA VOZ SIZE "MH"
TENOR	SELMER VI	'68	GUARDALA METAL "STUDIO"	GUARDALA	GUARDALA #3 or VANDOREN #2.5 SELECT
SOPRANO	CONN-GOLD CURVED W/ HIGH "F" LEVER	'20'S	ROVNER DEEP "V" LF METAL - SIZE 8	ROVNER GRADIENT LM	VANDOREN #3, RICO ROYAL #3.5 or GUARDALA #4
SOPRANO	CONN-STRAIGHT W/ HIGH "F" LEVER NICKEL/SILVER/ GOLD CONSTRUCTION	'20'S	ROVNER DEEP "V" METAL-SIZE 8	ROVNER GRADIENT LM	VANDOREN #3, RICO ROYAL #3.5 OR GUARDALA #4
EW1	AKAI PROFESSIONAL EQI 3000		RUN THRU 3WI 3000m SOUND MODULE, PROTEUS/2 AND PROTEUS/3 DIGITAL SOUND MODULES (EWI - ELECTRONIC WIND INSTRUMENT)		
MICRO- PHONE SYSTEM	ACK C409		A SAMSON VHF-FM "DIVERSITY II" WIRELESS REMOVE SYSTEM - SAMSON TRANSMITTER & RECEIVER (MODEL SR22) WITH AN AKG C409 GOOSENECK CLIP ON MICRO- PHONE ATTACHED		

STACCATO

Lesson 11 deals with a technique which uses a strong staccato effect combined with musical notations of sixteenth notes followed by eighth notes. Some forms of dance music use this notation because it adds "lift" to the rhythm. This percussive style of clipping a note has been popular in many styles of saxophone performance.

Please refer to the tape at this time.

EXAMPLE 24

Some of the first popular recordings to feature this style included;	
1958	*Cannonball* by Duane Eddy (sax solo by Steve Douglas)
1958	*Yakety Yak* by The Coasters (sax solo by King Curtis)
1959	*Forty Miles Of Bad Road* by Duane Eddy (sax solo by Steve Douglas)
1959	*Charlie Brown* by The Coasters (sax solo by King Curtis)
1963	*Yakety Sax* by Boots Randolph

Photo by Susan McGlohon

Photo by Laura Mac

JOE McGLOHON

PROFESSIONAL EXPERIENCE

Nationally Released Recordings

READ MY MIND	REBA MCENTIRE	MCA	93	MULTI-PLATINUM
REBA MCENTIRE	GREATEST HITS VOL.II	MCA	93	MULTI-PLATINUM
IT'S YOUR CALL	REBA MCENTIRE	MCA	93	MULTI-PLATINUM
SWEET SIXTEEN	REBA MCENTIRE	MCA	89	GOLD
REBA LIVE	REBA MCENTIRE	MCA	90	PLATINUM
LEE ROY PARNELL	LEE ROY PARNELL	ARISTA	88	
HEART OF DIXIE	MOVIE SOUNDTRACK	A&M	88	
BRILLIANT CONVERSATIONALIST	T. GRAHAM BROWN	CAPITOL	87	
COME AS YOU WERE	T. GRAHAM BROWN	CAPITOL	88	
BUMPER TO BUMPER	T. GRAHAM BROWN	CAPITOL	90	
HEARTWOOD	HEARTWOOD	GRC	73	
NOTHIN' FANCY	HEARTWOOD	GRC	74	

TOURS

January 89 To Present	Reba McEntire	U.S., CANADA, EUROPE
April 86 to December 88	T. Graham Brown	U.S., CANADA, EUROPE
October 85 To April 86	Delbert McClinton	U.S.
July 85 To September 85	Billy Chinnock	U.S.

TELEVISION

- The Tonight Show
- Arsenio Hall
- Hot Country Nights
- One Life To Live
- Nashville Now
- Search For Tomorrow

STAGE PERFORMANCES

Delbert McClinton
Stevie Ray Vaughn and Double Trouble
The Fabulous Thunderbirds
George Thourogood
Charlie Sexton
Tanya Tucker
Rodney Dangerfield
Steve Earle
Dave Mason
Joe Ely

Vince Gill
John Hall / Orleans
Richie Havens
Reba McEntire
Gregg Allman
Dicky Betts
Steve Cropper
Will Lee
Levon Helm

INSTRUMENTS:
YAMAHA TENOR SAXOPHONE
SELMER MARK VI SOPRANO SAXOPHONE
EV SYSTEMS WIRELESS GS 1000
EV MODEL 408 MICROPHONE
DIGITECH / SMARTSHIFT
L.A. SAX PRO MODEL TENOR

MOUTHPIECES:
VAN DOREN T95 JUMBO JAVA
Bobby Dukoff 80 - Tenor
Rovner #10 Facing
Otto Link 7*
Yaginasawa #10 Alto

LIGATURES:
Rovner

REEDS:
Hempke - Tenor, Alto and Soprano 3

MONITOR DESK:
Harrison SM-5

EFFECTS:
Yamaha SPX-90II
DBX 903

MONITORS:
Future Sonics UHF Wireless
Stereo Ear Monitor
Aphex Dominator II Stereo Limiter

Myanna

Myanna attracted immediate attention as a respected multi-sax player from the first time she stepped out onto the stage. And now, with the formation of her own pop-jazz band simply called **"MYANNA"**, she continues to seduce audiences with her cutting edge performances. In fact, **"MYANNA"** recently received the award for "outstanding local jazz act" at the highly regarded <u>Boston Music Awards</u>.

Before forming her own band, **Myanna** played with a number of extremely popular Boston based bands, the most celebrated being "Girls' Night Out". Performing frequently throughout New England, "GNO" was chosen as one of the five finalists in <u>Musician Magazine's</u> 1986 "Best Unsigned Band in America" contest. Receiving a multitude of favorable reviews, **Myanna's** talent was consistently highlighted.

After leaving "GNO", **Myanna** immediately began working on material for the new band she was forming. By combining a variety of styles, her original work easily crosses the line between jazz and pop with occasional inter-jections of blues and funk.

The release of her premier CD on her own <u>Bridge City</u> Label, P. O. Box 258, Boston, MA 02130, is the result of three years of writing, rehearsing and performing. Produced by Teese Gohl, best known for his work with Carly Simon and on the sound track for the movie "Aliens III", this self entitled album contains an array of tunes that are pleasingly diverse. With several cuts hitting the airwaves, **"MYANNA'** has secured as high as the number four position on several New England area radio station play lists.

Superior playing, accomplished writing, and a simmering sax bring **Myanna** to the forefront of the current music scene.

EQUIPMENT

Tenor - Selmer Mark VI (167000) with Precision Crafted and Peter Ponzol M/P's and #3 - 3/12 Vandoren reeds.
Alto - Selmer MarkVI (69000) with Dave Guardala studio model M/P and #3 1/2 Java reeds.
Soprano - Yamaha YSS model with Claude Lakey 5* M/P and Rico Royal #3 1/2 reed.
Yamaha WX-7 wind controller, Yamaha TX81Z, Korg 03RW, Shure WM98 wireless microphone and ART DR-X multi effects processor.

BOOTS RANDOLPH

Boots Randolph, a premier Nashville session saxophonist, recorded *Yakety Sax* in 1963 which reached #35 on the Top 40 charts. He has recorded for **Elvis Presley, Brenda Lee, Al Hirt** and **Pete Fountain**. In 1978 he opened his own Boots Randolph's Supper Club in Printers Alley, Nashville where he is featured six nights a week with his seven piece band. Record albums include;

Boots Randolph's Yakety Sax
Hip Boots
More Yakety Sax
The Fantastic Boots Randolph
Boots With Strings
Sax-Sational
Voices and Strings
Sunday Sax
Sound of Boots
With Love
Boots & Stockings - Christmas
Yakety Revisited

Hit Boots "1970"
Boots With Brass
Homer Louis Randolph, III
The Great Hits of Today
Sentimental Journey
Country Boots
Cool Boots
Greatest Hits
Sax Appeal
Puts A Little Sax In Your Life
Party Boots
Boots - Boots Randolph

(Photo courtesy of **Ray Stevens and Clyde Records**, 1707 Grand Ave., Nashville, TN 37212. "Boots", record #CLP-7001. Photographer Slick Lawson.)

Billy Vaughn was born on April 12, 1919 in Glasgow, Kentucky. He organized the Hilltoppers vocal group in 1952. He was the music director for Dot Records and arranged and conducted recordings for Pat Boone, Gale Storm and The Fontane Sisters. Billy Vaughn had more Pop hits than any other orchestra leader during the Rock and Roll era.

1954	#2	*Melody of Love*
1955	#5	*The Shifting Whispering Sands*
1956	#37	*Theme from the Three Penny Opera*
1956	#18	*When the Lilacs Bloom Again*
1957	#10	*Raunchy*
1958	#5	*Sail Along Silvery Moon*
1958	#30	*Tumbling Tumbleweeds*
1958	#20	*La Palmona*
1959	#37	*Blue Hawaii*
1960	#19	*Look for A Star*
1961	#28	*Wheels*
1962	#13	*A Swingin' Safari*

Billy Vaughn's arrangements always featured saxophone harmony with a lead alto.

SPECIAL EFFECTS

"Special effects" feature unusual creations. The following demonstrations are not often heard. One effect is produced by either talking or screaming through the horn between notes of a solo. One of the most interesting and educational recordings featuring this technique is *Don Ellis At Fillmore*, Columbia #30242. Saxophonist **John Klemmer** plays an outstanding solo on *Excursion II* in which he incorporates this technique.

Another effect is created by playing an altissimo note or a regular note and moving all fingers rapidly up and down without any pre-organized pattern as illustrated on the tape. And, there is the key click, or pad pop, as it is sometimes called.

There are many other effects which can be utilized but we will leave it up to your imagination and creative ability to find them.

I hope this study guide will give you some inspiration and insight to help you improve your own rock and roll style. Who knows . . . perhaps one day you will find yourself in a studio backing a recording star. Maybe **you** will someday become a part of Rock and Roll Saxophone history.

RECOMMENDED BOOKS
Honkers and Shouters - the golden years of rhythm and blues by Arnold Shaw, Macmillan Publishing Company 1978.
The Rockin' 50's by Arnold Shaw, Da Capo Paperback, NY, NY.
Rock, Roll and Remember by Dick Clark and Richard Robinson Popular Library, NY, 1976.
Rock and Roll Saxophone - video - by Steve Douglas, published by Hot Licks
and purchased through the *MIX BOOKSHELF*, 6400 Hollis St., #12, Emeryville, CA 94608.

Exercises and Studies
Universal Method for the Saxophone by Paul de Ville Carl Fischer, Inc., NY 1908.
Developing a Personal Saxophone Sound by David Liebman,
Caris Music Services, RD7, Box 762G, Stroudsburg, PA 18360.

Recommended Magazines
Saxophone Journal, P. O. Box 206, Medfield, Mass 02052.
down beat, 180 W. Park Ave., Elmhurst, IL 60126.
Windplayer, P. O. Box 15753, North Hollywood, CA 91615-9913.

JR. WALKER

Junior Walker (born Autry DeWatt) was born in Blytheville, Arkansas, in 1938. In 1958 he moved to South Bend, Indiana where he was inspired on alto and tenor sax by **George Mason, Gene Ammons, Louis Jordan, Earl Bostic** and **Illinois Jacquet**. He has a special respect for **Charlie Parker** and Nashville sessionman **Homer 'Boots' Randolph**. Legendary hits include;

1965	**#4**	*Shotgun*
1965	**#36**	*Do The Boomerang*
1965	**#43**	*Cleo's Back*
1965	**#29**	*Shake And Fingerpop*
1966	**#20**	*I'm A Road Runner*
1966	**#18**	*How Sweet It Is (To Be Loved By You)*
1966	**#50**	*Cleo's Mood*
1967	**#31**	*Pucker Up Buttercup*
1967	**#24**	*Come See About Me*
1968	**#31**	*Hip City - Part 2*
1969	**#41**	*What Does It Take (To Win Your Love)*
1969	**#16**	*These Eyes*
1970	**#21**	*Gotta Hold On To This Feeling*
1970	**#32**	*Do You See My Love (For You Growing)*

Photo courtesy **Motown Record Corporation**. From the LP *Jr. Walker & The All Stars* "Superstar Series" Volume 5.

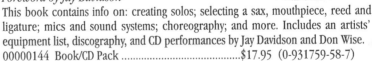